Reflections of a Priest
in a Time of Pain and Privilege

Patrick Bergquist

The Long Dark Winter's Night

The Long Dark Winter's Night

Reflections of a Priest in a Time of Pain and Privilege

Patrick Bergquist

LITURGICAL PRESS
Collegeville, Minnesota

www.litpress.org

1   2   3   4   5   6   7   8   9

Library of Congress Cataloging-in-Publication Data

Bergquist, Patrick.
    The long dark winter's night : reflections of a priest in a time of pain and privilege / Patrick Bergquist.
        p. cm.
    Includes bibliographical references (p.   ).
        ISBN 978-0-8146-3301-4
    1. Child sexual abuse by clergy—Meditations.   2. Catholic Church—Clergy—Sexual behavior—Meditations.   3. Priesthood—Catholic Church—Meditations.   4. Bergquist, Patrick.   I. Title.

BX1912.9.B44   2010
282.09'045—dc22   2009035528

To the Good People of St. Raphael Parish in Fairbanks, Alaska
who so patiently indulged me as a Poet
who so challenged me to be a Prophet
but most of all
who taught me how to be a Pastor

Contents

Acknowledgments

*A*s a priest I readily confess to a life of giving thanks at the table. As a believer I must confess that my heart continually gives thanks for the gentle and unassuming faith first taught me by my mother Mary and my father John—a faith I also shared with my brother John and my sisters Leslie, Kate, Beth, Sue, and Emily. As a pastor I also must confess that even my dreams give thanks for the wonderful years of ministry that I shared with Gloria Slagle. And as I writer I give words of thanks to Sherry Pappert, who so patiently listened to me when I first began to write; to Nancy Jackson, who with gentle compassion helped to edit what I first dared to write; to Marjorie Cole, who, as we sat around her table, helped me see myself as a writer with something to say; and to Liturgical Press, for believing that my words might actually have something to say for our church. To all of these, and to so many more—thank you.

Patrick Bergquist

Confessing to Winter's Night

A s I gaze out my frost-laden window, with its panes—my pains—graced in such delicate design, I find myself meditating and musing on the so-called new springtime in the Roman Catholic Church and its priesthood. And thus I find myself pondering what promises to be another seemingly endless winter. For when you find yourself lost in the depths of a deep dark winter, springtime can seem so very far away. It may be inevitable then, like the coming of winter itself, that enough time has passed, enough things have happened, for me to pause and peer out my window and at last attempt to put things into perspective—my church, my priesthood, and perhaps a bit of my life as well. And though I have searched endlessly, I can find no voice other than my own that dares to speak of, not a "new springtime," but a "long dark winter's night." How I wish and long that it was spring. But how can I, how can anyone, ignore the deepening winter outside?

I am but a simple parish priest, no saint and surely no scholar. I cannot and would not ever dare lay claim to any real authority or academic standing. My vantage point, the window from which I am blessed to see, is my parish and its wounded but wonderful people. What I do lay claim to is the lived reality of nearly twenty winters ordained, fifteen of them serving in the Missionary Diocese of Northern Alaska, a place where the number of winters spent is precisely how we mark the passing of time. Being in this place I can testify that winter is real, and it's enduring, and more often than not it's a struggle just to survive.

When I first came to Alaska in the fall of 1995, I did not know what to expect. At first I was tempted, as so many people are, to imagine myself wrapped up in a nice, warm hand-stitched quilt, safe and secure, with a stack of really good thick novels piled high beside me, waiting out the winter. As the current clergy sex abuse crisis and scandal in the Roman Catholic Church continues to linger and linger on, much like the long winter's night, I wonder how many of us have been tempted to do the very same—to wrap ourselves in the warm blanket of tradition and memory, all safe and secure, reading and re-reading through the stories of how wonderful things used to be, just biding our time, marking our place, hoping for spring. Yet the arctic winters are too long and too pervasive to wait out and pretend; and the cold dark nights outside our windows are too compelling to simply ignore. I wonder, though, if this is just what our church and our priesthood are doing in this moment of crisis and possible transformation: are we simply fooling ourselves that spring is around the corner and that once again things will return to what they used to be?

Here in the north I have come to discover and to truly appreciate that the long winter's night is the perfect place for both the poet and the prophet. Prophets are those who look deep into the very heart of the matter and dare to speak of the seriousness of the situation, speaking not from places of fear but out of faith. Poets, on the other hand, are those who fashion and form their words from deep within the human heart and experience—still deeper within the soul—giving voice to our hopes, our dreams, our fears, and our faith. If Dante had Virgil to guide him through purgatory, so we must rely upon the poets and the prophets to help and guide us through our long dark winter's night.

While I write this book for no other reason than to give voice to my own heart and soul, I do pray that others might at least give my voice a hearing, perhaps daring to see things as they are, or at least as I believe them to be. This is not, however, a book on the legitimacy or merits of the discipline of celibacy. Nor is it a treatise on church structures—for good or for bad—or an indictment of church leadership. What it is, at least what I hope and pray it to be, is a glimpse into the heart and soul of a parish priest struggling to make sense of a desperate situation.

For nothing is more dangerous and despairing here in the north than to simply ignore the seriousness of the situation, wishing it just wouldn't be so. Many may choose not to believe in this seriousness, this winter; but I challenge you to look out your window and ask yourself what it is that you see. As for me, I believe the so-called new springtime in our church—in my church—is still a long way off. Furthermore, I fear that our winter's night is barely half spent. I believe this crisis, this moment of transformation for our church, is real, and it is enduring. And like the winter's night, it too will cause us to struggle just to survive.

The long winter's night resounds with the songs of the poets. Robert Service dares to ask:

> Have you known the Great White Silence,
> > not a snow-gemmed twig aquiver?
> > > (Eternal truths that shame our soothing lies.)[1]

If ever you have stood alone in a forest on a cold winter night, so alone that not even the wind—not even the whispering through the trees—accompanies you, you would have no doubt heard the "Great White Silence." In this book I want to share with you some of the things that I have heard in that silence. Even as I do, I wonder why others have not heard, maybe even cannot hear. Possibly it takes someone living in the midst of the "Great White Silence" to truly describe what winter is.

A few winters past I wrote an article titled "A Long Winter's Night." In many ways this book grew out of that article, only more so. At that time, I wondered if we might find some sort of solace or sense of purpose in the clergy sex abuse crisis in light of the great mystic John of the Cross—and most especially in his *Dark Night of the Soul*. What I wrote then I still believe today: "When the road ahead disappears into darkness and all the familiar signs and symbols to which we have clung for security and familiarity are denied us, then and only then will we be ready to receive God's self-communication to our souls and perhaps to the soul of the priesthood."[2] Maybe St. John's *Dark Night* and Robert Service's "Great White Silence" are one and the same. And maybe, if we but dare, from deep within the very heart and soul of this silence—this darkness—we can still hear the voice of God. Truly this is my hope and my prayer.

During these long winter's nights I often find myself sitting by my window, reading through things that I wrote earlier in various journals, poems, and sermons, words penned in the deep dark silence.

> I have prayed that this darkness would have
> somehow dissipated and this Dark Night would
> have simply exhausted itself. But if anything it's
> only deepened and settled into the church's
> corporate soul. And still the shadows of broken
> innocence lay scattered and strewn along life's

wayside; like so many discarded dreams. Perhaps,
just yet maybe—it is darkest before the dawn.

It is here, and really, can only be here, where our journey through the long dark winter's night must begin—in the darkest hour before the dawn, in the winter
before the spring. With our innocence squandered, our
dreams all but shattered, and our priesthood suffering
(though I am finding many who disagree), do we yet
dare to venture forth into the darkness and the silence?
Yet even as we prepare to do so, we ought never to forget that here in this darkness and silence there is great
beauty, profound truth, and things that cause the soul to
simply stand in awe of it all. Contrary to popular belief,
the "Great White Silence" is not some empty wasteland,
nor is the "Dark Night" necessarily without sight. The
poet Theodore Roethke reminds us:

> In a dark time, the eye begins to see.
> I meet my shadow in the deepening shade.[3]

Have you ever seen the northern lights dance in the win-
tery night sky? If not, just listen then to the poet beckon:

> Let us probe the silent places, let us seek what luck
>   betide us;
> Let us journey to a lonely land I know.
> There's a whisper on the night-wind, there's a star
>   agleam to guide us."[4]

I ask that you join me here in the long dark winter's night. Listen to what I have seen and heard. Together we might come to find something of real purpose and meaning. Not just for ourselves but also, and most especially so, for those who venture here after us.

Chapter One

The Warning Winds of Winter

The Telltale Signs of Winter

Winter rarely, if ever, begins all at once, fully revealing itself to anyone foolish enough to inhabit it. False starts are many, often luring us and tempting us to question the actual beginning and ending of such seasons. Nevertheless, there are certain telltale signs that winter looms somewhere nearby, perhaps just over the horizon. A cold wind sweeps down from somewhere unseen. It appears without warning and from seemingly out of nowhere. It wraps itself around us and seeps deep into our bones. It awakens some long-forgotten instinct buried deep within us, buried in the very marrow of our memory, beckoning us to prepare and make ready. To make ready, if for no other reason than we might survive the approaching winter, preparing for the long cold darkness that will soon and inescapably surround us. If only we would heed its calling.

Soon after the wind, we awaken to the first hard-killing frost. Yes, there are always a few flirting frosts that come and go, and that are easily enough dismissed from our memories when the sun begins to warm our faces. However, the first really hard frost is of a different sort. While it might be beautiful to look at, there is also something strangely foreboding about it, for it brings with it a certain dying. The once bright and scenic leaves of autumn now fade from all their glory, turning to a dull and listless brown, even as they release their desperate and futile hold and drift away upon the wind. Flowers that once adorned our lives, enlivening our imaginations and reminding us of that garden of an original innocence now seemingly lost to us, wither and die. The first hard frost, like the cold north wind, leaves an undeniable and indelible mark upon the land-scape of our souls. As it has, I fear, upon the soul of our priesthood. Try as we might there is no denying it, there is no ignoring the approaching winter, even with all our talk of spring.

I first encountered the cold north wind and the kill-ing frost as a young, newly ordained East Coast priest, long before I would inevitably venture north and come to know the true depths of an arctic winter. It was the early 1990s, and I was just thirty years of age and still so full of dreams. I believe I was in love with the idea, with the notion, of being a priest; but never could I have known its true sacrifices. I could not have begun to imagine that it was my soul needing saving, my church needing redeeming.

I remember, what now seems nearly a lifetime ago, sitting amid a roomful of black suits and Roman collars. Looking back, I suppose these clergy meetings would have been encouraging and supporting experiences for a newly ordained priest such as myself (with the scent of fresh chrism still clinging to the palms of my hands). And I suppose these meetings could have been truly edifying had we gathered to share our lives as ministers of the Gospel and shepherds of God's people. But such was not the cause, nor the case, for gatherings such as these. It was not the cardinal or even his bishops who stood front and center before us, but rather six diocesan lawyers. These lawyers pointed out, point by meticulous point, what would happen to us should any of us find ourselves accused of certain "clerical improprieties" or "priestly misconduct with a minor"—and indeed, this was exactly how we spoke of such things way back when. And so it was that the clergy sex abuse scandal blew its way into our lives and came to settle upon our souls. Well, mine at least.

As I attempt to recall these events, even while still trying so desperately to separate them from my own innocence lost, I vividly remember the lawyers preaching as they pointed out across this sea of black suits and Roman collars: "When any of you find yourselves accused, know that an investigation will immediately ensue." This investigation, they assured us, need not necessarily be exhaustive or even conclusive. If, however, there seemed to be the slightest of hints, the slightest of suggestion that something inappropriate might have happened, then this would be sufficient grounds for an immediate suspension from active ministry. No questions asked. We all sat there stunned. Can anyone prove their innocence? Is it even possible? How did all of this come to be? And why? Little could we have known, although there are those who insist that we should have known. But as to the sheer depths and depravity of the situation, we just did not know. Many years later we would indeed come to know and understand, but at that time we didn't even dare to imagine, at least I didn't.

Following "credible accusation," the lawyers continued, civil and state authorities would be given our names. Then we would be sent off for psychological evaluation. It was at this time that words like *pedophilia* and *ephebophilia* first crept into our priestly lexicon. But honestly, we never knew where our accused brother priests were sent. They simply vanished. Gone too were their faculties and the license to practice their "craft and their trade." They were, as we would soon come to say, "removed from ministry," wherever and whatever that might actually mean. I guess for many of us sitting in the room that day, had we actually then been able to talk about it, it must have seemed as if we were living through some modern-day inquisition.

Strangely enough, what I most remember about those days were the *faxes*. Remember that these were the days before e-mail, cell phones, and text messaging. Faxes were the most expeditious way for the chancery offices to get out the official word of an accused brother priest. And so, I guess, in order not to be scooped by the local papers or embarrassed by the evening news, faxes soon began arriving from the chancery's office. And they kept coming, day after day, night after night. Many nights I would find myself waking to the distinct ring of the fax machine downstairs, both it and myself groaning and fearing—no, not again.

After the faxes came the bishops, with their hearts weighing heavy, to be sure. The bishops came to our parishes, not to preach the Good News, but to deliver the bad. They climbed into the once-ornate and glorious pulpits of our churches, not to proclaim "glad tidings to the lowly, to heal the broken hearted, to proclaim liberty to the captives and release to the prisoners" (Isaiah 61:1), but rather to inform Christ's holy people that their shepherd, their pastor, their priest had been accused of unspeakable crimes against innocence and against children. Further, the bishops told the people that they, the faithful if not fearful flock, were obligated (certainly a word near and dear to all Catholics) under both civil and ecclesiastical law to come forward if they had any information concerning this priest, or for that matter, any other priest. It was truly a day when a cold wind swept down from somewhere unseen, and quite literally blew us priests off our pedestals, all the while the faithful sat in their pews stunned, almost beyond belief.

As for my brother priests, now forever branded with the new scarlet letters *PP*, Pedophile Priest (two words that in time would come to be considered nearly synonymous with one another)—they were consigned and forsaken to aimlessly wander about in a new sort of ecclesiastical limbo, rarely if ever to be heard of again. Occasionally, we caught a fleeting glimpse of them on the evening news as they were paraded off in handcuffs. But mostly, and sad to say, they just slipped away from our sight, from our collective memories, never to be heard from or spoken of again. Or so we at least prayed.

What amazes me most about these early days of the clergy sex abuse crisis was the sheer lack of any faith talk, God talk. And really, God would play little or no part in these proceedings, except perhaps in the final judgment in the end. As I look back on these events now, I believe that the church, my church, simply chose the courtroom over its confessions, its contrition, and its convictions. All this seemed my church's veiled and desperate attempt to save the institution and to protect its priesthood. But, I ask, to what end? This desperate attempt appeared to be the "sole," but not necessarily the "soul," issue at hand. And still I ask myself why the church chose to react out of fear but, sadly, never chose to act out of faith. And, to be perfectly honest about it, I believe the church has yet to do so even now. What is it that we as church pray each Lent?

> *For I acknowledge my offense,*
>   *and my sin is before me always:*
> *"Against you only have I sinned,*
>   *and done what is evil in your sight." . . .*
> *My sacrifice, O God, is a contrite spirit;*
>   *a heart humbled and contrite O God, you will not*
>   *spurn.*

(see Psalm 51:5-6, 19)

In a world filled with "what ifs"—What if the church, my church, had actually practiced what she preached? What if the church had herself confessed its sins and pleaded for forgiveness? What if . . . ? One only has to wonder how things might be different today.

I have witnessed with my own eyes, indeed with my own broken heart, men I once knew, or thought I knew, men I had admired and revered, now bound and shackled. Men of the cloth clothed now in the bright orange jumpsuits of prison-yard garb. Jesus forewarned Peter: "Amen, amen, I say to you, when you were younger, you used to dress yourself and go where you wanted; but when you grow old, you will stretch out your hands, and someone else will dress you and lead you where you do not want to go" (John 21:18). Jesus said this to Peter, however, not because of Peter's sin but because this was the true cost of discipleship. These men, on the other hand, these men I once held as living examples of faithful ministry and holy priesthood, now stood disfigured in disgrace and shackled in their shame. What must a vision such as this do to the mind and heart of a newly ordained priest? What sort of spiritual scars must my generation carry upon our souls?

I do confess that there is indeed a scar left upon my soul when I contemplate my priesthood, my church—not because of how things ought to be but because of how things really are. How best can I describe this scar to you? Perhaps a story might help. As I have said, winters in Alaska are very long. It seems they begin around September and rarely end much before May. As a result, people do a myriad of things just to occupy their time as they wait for spring. I am convinced that one of the things we do as a community, and that we seem to enjoy most, is to argue. Because winter is so long we need something, anything really, to argue about. It doesn't matter what the issue or controversy may be, and, in fact, come spring we usually just forget whatever it was we were arguing about. Over the winter, though, the editorial page of our local paper makes for some interesting reading, most especially the letters to the editor. In these letters there is a friendly, though sometimes not so friendly, bantering back and forth.

So when a number of articles concerning the priest sex abuse scandal began to appear in our local paper, you could expect there were going to be some letters in response. And so there were, back and forth. Some praised the priesthood, some condemned the priesthood. But the one letter I remember most was one that likened the priesthood to being an "Icon of Christ." Who could argue with something like this? Well, this might be true in a perfect world, but not so in mine. Being a priest, I felt somewhat compelled to write something in response. But I confess that I lacked the courage to actually send it. Then again, perhaps what I wrote then best belongs here, in a place such as this, within the settings of a deeper conversation:

> Recently in the letters to the editor there have been references to the Roman Catholic priesthood as being an "Icon of Christ." In many ways this is a wonderful and noble analogy of what will always remain but a mystery. In my understanding, limited though it may be, when praying with an icon a person looks through the painted and gilded image as if it were a window to something beyond, perhaps to a small glimpse of heaven itself. The image is of incidental importance when compared with the revealed wisdom, grace, and beauty of the divine that lies therein.

> I, for myself, carry a deep and bleeding wound within my heart and soul as I contemplate this icon of the priesthood. Not of how things should be, but of how things are. The icon

through which I look is not made of gilded gold but resembles more a shattered and broken window, seeking only to distort and disfigure the figure of Christ. Priests accused and even convicted of unspeakable crimes against innocence. But speak of them we must. Those who have violated both body and soul—men, brothers I once knew, respected, and admired—now shackled and disgraced. Did I know them at all? This is the icon with which much of our society now views the priesthood.

Looking back on the years I have been a priest, I begin to wonder whether the crucifix is not a more authentic image on which to meditate and pray, whether the tortured and contorted face of Christ is a more realistic portrayal of how things are, with one notable exception—his innocence, our guilt. Not an icon of a resurrected Christ, but one of a crucified Christ. Blame not the victims, or the media, or the lawyers, or the courts. In truth, this is a *self-inflicted crucifixion* and a tragedy of our own making. For who would dare paint such a picture? And who would dare look through such a window?

Who would paint such a picture? I guess I would. Who would dare to look through such a window? I guess I must. But still I must ask why my church or my brother priests will not dare to look through this shattered pane. This very realization was perhaps the beginning of my own long winter's night, the one that I now see outside my window.

Though I did not send that letter to the editor, I could not remain silent. Each Friday our paper has a "Faith Page" that covers anything from the election of a pope to a potluck supper at one of our local churches. One regular feature of this page is the Insight Column, a place where local pastors are invited to write words of inspiration and hope for our community. Given this opportunity, and having impatiently waited for someone of more authority and importance than myself to write something, anything really, I wrote this back in 2003:

> It's been twelve years now since sacred hands were laid upon my head and my own hands were anointed with the blessed oil, and I was ordained a Roman Catholic Priest. I began my journey with innocence, perhaps a bit naive, believing in the goodness of God's promise. I believed then, and still do today, in the incredible potential of the human heart for things of beauty and grace. But what I have seen, indeed what we are all just now beginning to see, is also the capacity of the human heart for things of ugliness and sin.
>
> As a Catholic Priest I am embarrassed, angered, even horrified as I hear of new and ever-increasing revelations of children abused and victimized by

my brother priests. A child's innocence stolen, their faith betrayed. And the institution of the church, my church, only perpetuating and participating in this sin by its silence or complicity for years and years. This same institution that I once promised my solemn obedience to, and that for the salvation of my soul. It is enough to make a poor parish priest cry out in anguish.

Twelve years ago now I stepped out in faith; with nothing but the promises of God's love I sought to find hope where I could, and where I could not, to bring that hope which God so freely bestows. The Roman collar that I wore around my neck was never anything to boast in, but rather was my gift to God, a sign and symbol of a life freely given—mind, body, and soul. Today that same collar, frayed a bit from wear, is a source of shame and disgrace. The violence of others reflecting back upon me. As I look into the beautiful innocent eyes of a child, the one place in all creation where truly anything is possible, and all good things can be imagined, I cannot but help to see the face of my God. How could anyone, let alone a priest, violate something so sacred, so holy?[5]

Throughout the 1990s I hoped and prayed that a revealing wind would blow through the church and stir up our souls. I hoped that all this would awaken in us some long-forgotten notion of what it means to be church, what it means to be priest. But, sad to say, it did not. A cold north wind assaulted us, but we dismissed it, believing that the worst had passed us by. That somehow we had weathered the storm and life would once again return to how it used to be. We convinced ourselves that people would just forgive and forget, and we could again be deserving of their respect and the respect due our holy office. The long dark winter's night, however, is not so easily dismissed, and the true depth of winter's chill had yet to reach or pierce our hearts or our souls. Yes, a cold north wind blew into our lives, but we chose to turn our faces and ignore the coming winter. As William Shakespeare forewarned and foretold:

> Blow, blow, thou winter wind.
> Thou are not so unkind
>   As man's ingratitude. [6]

In the Fullness of Winter

Winter finally arrived in earnest. Settling first in Boston, then Dallas, and finally, inevitably and ironically, with ever-new revelations of abuse, it arrived here in Alaska. Looking back upon winter's arrival I soon found myself writing:

> The snow outside is gently falling as I sit and
> begin to write what is in my heart and soul. So

often, here in this seemingly remote corner that we call Alaska, we can pretend that the world outside does not really exist, that it is all just something we watch on CNN, far removed and full of make believe. The current crisis in the Catholic Church has been slow in coming to us, but then again it takes awhile for things like the mail to reach us. . . . But if the truth be known, no cold, no ice, no wall of isolation could separate us from the rest of the church—neither its sins nor its sufferings.[7]

We had sighed so heavily, had so sincerely believed we'd survived the worst of it. We'd weathered the storm. But we were sadly mistaken, and soon enough we awoke to find our priestly sins splashed all over the front pages of the *Boston Globe*, the *New York Times*, and yes, even the *Fairbanks Daily News-Miner*. No, they hadn't just forgotten. Nor did it seem they had forgiven. How could anyone really forget? And as for their forgiveness, this was going to cost us more than we ever dared imagine or even pray.

Winter usually arrives with a certain rudeness. It is not usually anxiously awaited or anticipated like the other seasons of the year. It is almost always nearly dreaded. In the north we even add two more seasons: "freeze-up" and "break-up." Freeze-up occurs when the streams and rivers, ponds and lakes, and even the seas themselves wrap themselves in the white baptismal garments of ice and snow, though for some it might seem more a funeral pall (the white cloth that drapes over a casket). The waters' depths, their currents, their lives, remain hidden from late September until May, and sometimes even well into June, when all of a sudden they throw off their heavy cloaks of ice and snow, and are resurrected, sometimes most violently so in break-up. But break-up in the north isn't the new springtime. It is summer, and summer is the stuff of yet another story.

For now it is winter, and as I have said, I fear our winter is barely half spent. It is here in the midst and depths of winter that the prophets do dwell. These prophets, like winter itself, speak with a certain crass rudeness. They speak, and at first we are intrigued, perhaps even fascinated. Their mystical presence captivates us. But when the truth of their words, like a two-edged sword, begins to pierce deep into our hearts, we find them—much like a long winter—utterly too much to bear.

How well I remember my first winter in Alaska. To the new and uninitiated there's a certain fascination that captivates the imagination, just staring at the thermometer with its red line falling. Watching it fall past the point of freezing, not hesitating at zero but slipping ever deeper to ten, twenty, thirty, forty, even fifty degrees below. For the new and the naive this first winter is full of wonder and awe. It's even cause to boast to family and friends living somewhere warmer. But come the second or third winter, the novelty, much like the linings of our parkas and the soles of our boots, wears a bit thin—as does our patience. I suppose in this way winter is like the prophets, and prophets, like the winter. Fascinating at first, even somewhat captivating, but when the icy truth of their words shatters our illusions, we find them too much to bear.

Prophets seem to belong to a different era, a different time, and a distant place. But here in the midst of the long winter's night, they are at home. There is a certain clarity in the stillness of the winter air, which makes it the perfect place for the poet and the prophet. When winter finally and firmly embraces you and you become aware of the very breath inside of you, now made visible in the mist before your eyes, there is no denying its reality. When your every footfall in the snow makes you aware of your aloneness and the beating of your heart becomes something almost tangible, there is no denying winter's presence. And it is here, in this place, that the prophets have chosen to pitch their tent. As I said, prophets look into the heart of the matter and speak of the seriousness of the situation. They speak not out of fear but out of faith. And if perchance I remember the lessons of seminary correctly, prophets are not so much fortune tellers as they are tellers of the truth. They are not so much soothsayers as they are sayers and seers of the truth. They do not so much look into tomorrow as they peer and pierce into today. And this could be why we fear them so.

I realize I am probably very much alone in believing this. I believe that we as church owe a deep debt of gratitude to the press and the media, strange as that might seem. For when we could not, when we would not face our inner demons, they dared to show them to us. When we lacked the integrity due our calling, they demonstrated the relentless commitment of theirs. When we lost our prophetic voice, imparted to us on the day of our baptism—called forth from us on the day of our ordination—they found theirs, all the while we fearfully clung to our silence. And while the media might not have gotten everything exactly right, they nonetheless did their level best. (We need always to remember that ours is a church not easily given to full disclosure.) When we needed to be prophets, even within the very mess we had created, we couldn't be, we wouldn't be. Perhaps we were like the prophet Jonah and simply chose to turn and flee from our appointed Nineveh. In the end, like Jonah, we simply could not run away from ourselves.

The *Boston Globe* is often heralded, and I suppose rightly so, for being the voice that broke the story. I wonder, however, if the full story has yet been told. When the *Globe* was awarded the 2003 Pulitzer Prize in Public Service journalism, it was commended for its "courageous, comprehensive coverage of sexual abuse by priests, an effort that pierced secrecy, stirred local, national and international reaction and produced changes in the Roman Catholic Church." How I wish it were true. Instead, I am left wondering whether these "changes in the Roman Catholic Church" will ever truly be realized. Was this true *metanoia*, or change of heart, on behalf of my church, or was it merely a placation to forces beyond its control? All the while we just waited out the storm, waited for things to blow over, waited for everything to return to how they used to be. The church, my church, has always been terrified of change.

In the winter of 2004 Bishop Wilton Gregory, then president of the United States Conference of Catholic Bishops, presented the John Jay College study *The Nature and Scope of the Problem of Sexual Abuse of Minors by Catholic Priests and Deacons in the United States*, which had been commissioned by the newly formed National Review Board. Bishop Gregory began his presentation with this most remarkable line: "The terrible history recorded here today is history." Oh, how I wish that were true. The words of philosopher George Santayana come to mind: "Those who cannot remember the past [history] are condemned to repeat it." And so the horrid revelations of the 1990s were once again resurrected in the new days of the new millennium.

As the fax machine gave way to the internet so too did my perspective grow. From the window of my lap-

top my eyes were opened wide by web sites such as
Abuse Tracker: "A digest of links to media coverage of
clergy abuse. Click on the headline to read the full
story."[8] Each day this site reveals the many tragic stories
that make up this crisis, not just in Alaska but all over the
Catholic world. To many people in the pews, indeed to
many parish priests just struggling to get through the
crisis, it might seem as if Bishop Gregory's words—
"[this] history. . . is history"—are prophetic. But to
those who look through the window of "Abuse Tracker"
and read the stories contained therein, it is quite obvious
this is not the case. Each day these windows open to re-
veal more of the sordid and horrid truth. View this, and
many other similar sites, and you soon realize that our
church is still bleeding, our winter is far from over, and
the new springtime is indeed a long way off. Each day
the prophets prophesy, the reporters report, and each day
my church dies just a little more.

The long winter's night is a deep and abiding place,
but the press and the media are not the only voices to
be heard here. Journalists, I am convinced, became the
prophets of this scandal almost by default; but there
were other voices crying out in this wilderness as well.
As early as 1985 Thomas Doyle, OP, Michael Peterson,
MD, and Mr. F. Ray Mouton, JD, had cried out to the
"seriousness of the situation." They presented a paper
to our bishops, *The Problem of Sexual Molestation by
Roman Catholic Clergy: Meeting the Problem in a*

Comprehensive and Responsible Manner—this, nearly twenty years prior to the John Jay College study. But did anyone hear them or take them to heart? Did anyone heed the prophets' cry or harken to the seriousness of the situation? The Mouton-Doyle-Peterson Report, as it would come to be known, begins with this most haunting line: "Some extremely serious issues have arisen that presently place the church in the posture of facing extremely serious financial consequences as well as significant injury to its image."[9]

Knowing all this, having been warned of all of it back in 1985, how is it that we still wonder how we got to where we are today? To tell the truth, we are even a bit surprised by it all. And to be brutally honest, many have just simply grown weary of it all. Didn't Jesus say to the would-be disciples, "let the dead bury their dead" (Luke 9:60)? Why, we priests cry, why can't we bury this too? Why? Because the death of our illusions comes by way of acceptance, not by way of denial. I believe in the depths of my heart and soul that we have yet to accept or to embrace our long winter's night. Instead, we choose to distract ourselves from winter's humbling demands with all our talk of spring, a new springtime at that. All the while the world looks at us in sheer and utter disbelief.

Where once I thought I could wait out winter, sitting by my window, wrapped in a quilt, a pile of good novels beside me, it just hasn't worked out that way.

There is, to be sure, a pile of books beside my chair, falling over due to its ever-increasing numbers. A random view of their titles reads like some sort of pathological nightmare: *Our Fathers: The Secret Life of the Catholic Church in an Age of Scandal* by David France; *A Gospel of Shame: Children, Sexual Abuse, and the Catholic Church* by Frank Bruni and Elinor Burkett; *Sex, Priests, and Secret Codes: The Catholic Church's 2000-Year Paper Trail of Sexual Abuse* by Thomas Doyle, A.W. Richard Sipe, and Patrick Wall; *Lead Us Not into Temptation: Catholic Priests and the Sexual Abuse of Children* by Jason Berry; *Sex, Priests, and Power: Anatomy of a Crisis* by A.W. Richard Sipe; *Children Left Behind: The Dark Legacy of Indian Mission Boarding Schools* by Tim Giago; *Sacrilege: Sexual Abuse in the Catholic Church* by Leon Podles; *An Irish Tragedy: How Sex Abuse by Irish Priests Helped Cripple the Catholic Church* by Joe Rigert—and many, many others. These are the prophetic voices of those who have peered into the darkness of winter's night. And they too have given us the voices of those who seem to have no voice, whose innocence we stole, and whose souls we raped. The voices of the victims' souls who still cry out in the wilderness, pleading to be heard. And I promise we will hear them, for truly there's something healing in the telling of their stories.

SNAP's (Survivors Network of those Abused by Priests) mission statement reads: "By sharing our stories, we recognize that we are not alone, and we are not guilty for what happened to us. Gradually coming to a full knowledge of this empowers us to confront the truth, and to find healthy mechanisms for healing."[10] The shadows of broken innocence will not, cannot, simply be left scattered and strewn along life's wayside, like so many discarded dreams.

Listen, then, to the long winter's night calling. Listen carefully to the "Great White Silence." There is a most conspicuous voice missing, strangely silent among the sad and often angry, lamenting chorus. It is not that of the church's magisterium, or the lawyers, or the courts, or the journalists, or the social commentators and critics. It is not even the voice of the victims themselves. It is the voice of us parish priests. Scripture tells us that the prophet Jeremiah was thrown into a dry cistern in order to silence him from saying something others did not want to hear. Perhaps we parish priests just slipped and fell into this cistern and now stand in a hole in the ground, our feet stuck in the mud, choosing to be silent in our protest. Or maybe we have grown numb in the cold night and are unable or unwilling to speak. I have come to believe that we don't speak, we can't speak, simply because we are afraid. And it is our fear that has paralyzed us, causing our feet to be stuck and our tongues to be silent. In a winter such as this, what is needed is *faith*—not fear.

In this, the long winter of our self-inflicted crucifixion, too often we priests blindly lash out in fear at those we falsely believe to be the cause of all our pain: greedy lawyers, an overzealous media, and even those we have so grievously harmed. We believe in some sad and sordid way that all this is being done to us. We actually believe, we have somehow managed to convince ourselves, that priests are the true victims of this scandal. The pitiful and mournful cry I hear most often amid the sea of black suits and Roman collars echoes like some common dirge: *"Why are they doing this to me?"* ("They" meaning the lawyers, reporters, and victims themselves.) *"I've done nothing wrong!" "I am even afraid to wear my collar out in public."* And always: *"Why do they have to keep saying, 'Pedophile Priests'?"*

There are, of course, those in our ranks who attempt to resist the winter's night by self-righteously proclaiming the new springtime, by becoming more Catholic than the pope himself. These are the ones who boldly boast of their freshly starched Roman collars, who choose to see these collars as some sort of defiant badge of distinction, insisting that it is just a few bad apples who are responsible for all of this. These are the ones who tenaciously defend their priestly identities by overt acts of public piety, all the while being too busy praying to hear those who are weeping. I remember reading somewhere, but for the life of me cannot remember where, that *a truly spiritual person tries less to be holy than to be deeply human*. I cannot help but believe that the redemption of the Roman Catholic priesthood will be found not in our being "set apart" but in our solidarity with those who weep.

In our long winter's night certain existential questions have arisen concerning our priestly identity. In his groundbreaking and thought-provoking book, *The Changing Face of Priesthood*, Donald Cozzens writes:

> At the core of the priest's crisis of soul, then, is the search for this unfolding identity as an ordained servant of Jesus Christ. Behind and beyond issues of integrity and intimacy that shape the quality of his soul lies the lingering question of his true self as one ordained into the priesthood of the one High Priest. [11]

Our crisis of soul, both as individuals and as the corporate soul of the priesthood, has little to do with how things appear. It is about how thing are and ought to be. As I see it,

> the quest for a new priesthood, or perhaps the discernment of a more actualized priesthood in this dark night, lies not in the disparaging debates between *alter Christus* or *in persona Christi* but in the lived reality of the suffering and death of Christ—that one true and authentic priest from whom and with whom all meaning, purpose. and existence of priesthood must necessarily originate. The cries of those victimized at the hands of those who would pretend to be Christ are in fact the cries of Christ and therefore the

cries of the modern priesthood . . . even more
so they are the wounds of those brutalized—either
by sins of the flesh, sins of presumption, or
sins of just plain indifference—the wounds of
Christ and, therefore, also the wounds of the
priesthood.[12]

If ever the truth be told, the true victims of this scandal
are not we priests. The victims are those we have
harmed through our thoughts, words, and deeds. Those
we have injured by the sins of our commission or our
omission, in what we have done or what we have failed
to do. In truth, their pain and suffering shame ours.
This may be precisely what the poet Robert Service
intended when he wrote: "Eternal truths that shame
our soothing lies."

Listen, then, to the whispers upon winter's wind,
crying out like a prophet in the wilderness or a poet in
some barren wasteland.

Chapter Two

An Endless Winter of Discontent

There are times when prophets become poets and poets become prophets. In *The Sonnets to Orpheus* the poet Rainer Maria Rilke dares to prophesy:

> Be in advance of all parting, as though it were
>   behind you like the winter that is just going.
>   For among winters one is so endlessly winter
>   that, overwintering, your heart once for all
>   will hold out.[13]

To those who have been used and abused by my church, it must indeed seem an endless winter. I have found that here in the north it is not necessarily winter's cold, or even winter's darkness, that plagues and wearies the soul—but winter's duration, like some reoccurring nightmare that never ends. Sad to say, many here in the north are haunted by a seasonal depression, SAD (seasonal affective disorder). While this might be expected in the months of December or January or even February (all of which hold just a few precious hours of sunlight each day), this depression, I am told, usually settles deep within someone's soul in the months of March or April. With the warming of the air and the brightening of the sky, someone is easily lured and tempted into believing the end of winter is near. It is not, however, and sometimes it feels as if it never will be. So also the clergy or priest sex abuse scandal that lingers on like a nightmare that never seems to end. But what about those whose nightmares torment their every waking moment? What about those whose pain simply shames ours?

Here I must confess that I have never been abused by a priest, or by a nun, or by anyone else for that matter. I would never pretend to know the depths of this pain. Yet I have listened. I have listened to them tell their stories, and having listened, found myself weeping alongside of them. When no one would come to dry their tears, or bind their wounds, or simply just to say how sorry they were, their brokenness grew into anger. Who could really blame them? Strangely, perversely perhaps, my church can and still does blame them. I offer these stories not that someone's pain or shame be deepened or cheapened but to illustrate how this crisis of soul has come to change the heart of at least one priest—me. I plead with you to listen with me to the voices of those who cry out in the wilderness and apparent wasteland of our church. Hear their voices and share their stories. For it is only in the sharing of their stories, their agonizing heart-wrenching stories, that we priests might find purpose, meaning, and even healing in ours.

Sister Susanna and the Story of the Rape of Helpless Innocence

I first encountered this sin, this sadness, while still in the formative years of seminary, when I was so very young, so idealistic, so naive. It was my first winter of discontent, and it came, strangely enough, on a hot summer day. I remember, though I have tried to forget, sitting on the curb of a city street alongside a young nun, her face awash in tears. I will call her Sister Susanna of the Holy Innocence (I choose this pseudonym because she reminds me of the young woman who was shamed and discredited in chapter 13 of the book of Daniel). Sister Susanna, though an adult, in some ways seemed more like a child. She possessed that rare and precious gift of innocence that seems capable of believing only in the goodness of people, incapable of knowing a more sinister side of life.

And so it was that I sat there on that hot summer day, utterly and completely stunned as Susanna told me her tearful and heartbreaking story. It had happened late one night when she (who was at the time recovering from an accident) was convalescing in a Catholic rectory, something that had actually been my idea. How little did I know back then, how foolish and naive I was. In the months prior to her telling me her story, I had picked up Sister Susanna from a local hospital. Though still confined to a wheelchair and unable to walk, she had been declared by the hospital to be on the road to recovery. But since she lived alone and could not care for herself, I suggested Susanna stay in a parish I knew to be a place of great generosity and affirmation. I thought she too might find it a place of healing. It really did seem at the time, a simpler time, such a good idea. Looking back on things now, I cannot begin to forgive myself for my foolish mistake.

Back, then, to that hot summer day as I sat beside her on the curb and she told me of the nightmare she had endured. Late one night, after everyone had gone home, the parish priest raped her. I couldn't believe her story. I didn't want to believe her story. I didn't really know what to do, or what to believe. How could a priest—an *alter Christus* (another Christ)—do something like this? How could a priest—acting *in persona Christi* (in the person of Christ)—abuse, violate, and rape a helpless, partially paralyzed nun? At the time it did seem too much to believe. What Leon Podles writes is true: "The mystery of evil is made all the harder to bear when Satan wears a Roman collar."[14]

Setting my disbelief aside on that hot and humid day, I managed to get Sister to a local rape-crisis counseling center, where I hoped and prayed she might find some sort of healing. I did what I could and thanked God it was mercifully out of my hands. I could get back to my studies, so that one day I might become a priest. So, at least at that time I thought and prayed. Now, hindsight being 20/20, I know what I should have done. I should have called the police. Sad to say, I never did.

After the passing of a few weeks, or was it months, I received a call from Sister's counselor at the rape-crisis center, who asked if I would come in and speak with her. I reluctantly agreed, for in my heart of hearts I simply wanted no part of this. I felt ill prepared, ill equipped, and certainly ill at ease in dealing with a priest rapist and a nun who had been assaulted. After all, who was I? I was just a seminarian, trying desperately to become a priest. My world was small, just as it was innocent. It was still full of ideas and theories, and all this seemed quite beyond me. The counselor asked if I believed Sister Susanna. I said no. I could never imagine this priest committing such a horrific act. The counselor said that I must believe Susanna; but I rebelled at the demand, truly resenting having to believe her story. I wanted to believe. But, no, perhaps I did not want to after all. If I believed her story, then everything I knew, or at least thought I knew, about the priesthood, about my church could be called into question.

Years later it all would be. But at the time, my little world of seminary made sense to me; it was predictable, it was reasonable, and above all it, was safe. To believe something so shameful, so sinful, would have caused my safe little sanctuary to come crashing in like a house built of cards. In spite of it all, or maybe because of it all, I confronted the priest. But really, who was I—just a lowly seminarian—to question such a well-respected priest? He, of course, to no one's great surprise, denied everything. Sister was just making all this up, he said, all these seditious and slanderous lies. For years, I confess, I bought his side of the story over hers.

To my knowledge, no charges were pressed in this case and, for the most part, it was easy enough to dismiss these painful memories, all the while I got on with the business of being a priest. That is, until one day nearly twenty years later, when it all came flooding back. I received not one but two phone calls asking about those days long since past. The first came from a newspaper reporter doing background for a story on the case. The second was from a police officer asking the very same questions. I answered as I could, saying that I sincerely believed something did happen that night, oh so long ago; as to exactly what, I could not say, but I was sure something did happen. Finally and mercifully, I believed Sister. Really, I just had to.

Living in the north you become very aware of both the presence and the absence of light. Aware of not only its quantity but also its quality, as it shines, pierces, and steals its way into your heart. I am reminded of the poet Emily Dickinson's words:

There's a certain slant of light
On winter afternoons,
That oppresses, like the weight
Of cathedral tunes.

Heavenly hurt it gives us;
We can find no scar
But internal difference
Where the meanings are. [15]

In the land of the midnight sun, summer's light is all
pervasive, all consuming, as it chases the fleeting shadows of night. Yet in the winter, for months on end, it
fearfully seems as if the day has shamelessly surrendered
to the night. It is a trifling thing to gain or lose seven
minutes of sunlight per day—that is, of course, until
you consider that in a week's time it adds up to nearly
three quarters of an hour, and in a month, to nearly
three hours. Yes, there is a "certain slant of light," even
in the midst of the long winter's night. The sun's lowly
rising in the southern sky casts a certain light, trans-
forming an otherwise formless, shapeless night into a
work of art worthy of God. Painted in such delicate
pastels of pink, orange, and purple, it nearly defies de-
scription. There is a week or so come January when
from my window, the 20,000-foot-plus Mount
McKinley is backlit by the fading sun, and though it is
more than a hundred miles distant, it appears close
enough for me to reach out and hold it in the palm of

my hand. Most of the time, the closer you are to this awe-inspiring sight, the less likely you are to actually see it, but with a little distance and just the right light, it suddenly strikes upon your imagination and stirs your inmost soul.

The Story of Lazarus and Healing the Brokenhearted

The calendar hanging on my wall indicated it was nearly spring, just two weeks before the holiest of weeks. But outside my window it still looked very much like winter. I first met Lazarus (a pseudonym as well, one befitting someone whose life was once lost and later restored) late one afternoon over a cup of coffee. For months someone in the parish had been telling me I needed to meet this man. But I did not know why. He walked into the coffeehouse and looked around. I looked up and guessed, "Lazarus?" We exchanged the usual greetings, and he sat down across from me. He seemed a little tentative, a little nervous, but nonetheless he sat across from me as I went on and on about my supposed predicament. The clergy sex abuse crisis had finally and quite unabashedly come north to Alaska. Now no longer just a seminarian but a pastor, I knew that I needed to do something for my parish to make sense of this nightmare. Exactly what, I was not sure. I had preached about the pending crisis. I had invited people to stay after Mass and to share what was in their hearts. I had written articles for the papers and even letters to the bishop. But there remained something more I needed to do. I shared all this with Lazarus that day. But even as I spoke, hidden in the deep recesses of my mind were the ever-present worries and woes of the pending Holy Week. Yes, the paschal mystery lay heavy upon my heart that day.

When I finally ceased speaking, Lazarus looked intently at me and with tears in his eyes said, "You don't know my story, do you?" I never had suspected, or dared to imagine, he actually might have a story. In reality, though, who doesn't? Lazarus breathed deeply and asked me if I wanted to hear the story of a survivor. Only then did I begin to realize that I was sitting across the table from not just a victim but a survivor of this crisis. He proceeded to tell me his story, to tell me how he, now a grown man of fifty-plus years, had been violently raped and sodomized at the tender age of ten by a priest. We sat for what seemed hours as he carefully and gently unfolded his nightmare on the table between us. Over forty years had passed, but in his mind, it was just as if it were yesterday. He breathed deeper, never once taking his eyes off mine, and recounted how his pants were pulled down and the unspeakable things that followed. But speak of them we must. Lazarus told me that only by telling his story could he ever hope to claim some semblance of power over what had happened to him so long ago, only in the remembering could he heal. And sitting there in front of me was a man, fragile to be sure, but nonetheless healed.

After the unspeakable, the unimaginable, things that had happened to him, he remembered pulling up his pants and going outside to where his own unsuspecting father was waiting to take him home—his father not having the slightest inkling of what had just happened, and Lazarus, a ten-year-old boy, not able to tell him. Lazarus told me how his life would never, could never, be the same. He even shared with me a story of a recent doctor's appointment. He told me that even now he needed the reassurance of his doctor that he was in fact going to be safe. He told his doctor what had happened to him and that, though he was a grown man, he always needed to ensure the safety of that little ten-year-old boy inside, the one who had been raped by a priest. He told me that all throughout his adult life he always needed to make absolute certain that this little boy inside was safe from any harm.

How many times we hear people, my own brother priests, say the victims should just get over it; it happened so long ago. Can we not see the ten-year-old boy, so brutally and violently abused, who still cries out in our midst? Do we *not* want to see him?

The death of Lazarus's innocence, at the hands of a supposedly holy man, was a life story of struggle and eventual triumph over evil. Yet tragically, the church of

Lazarus's childhood never uttered its own contrition or sorrow, nor would it ever accept and own up to its responsibility. The priest who raped Lazarus would go on to be "creditably accused" by hundreds of others whose lives, whose childhoods, whose very souls he stole. Many years later, he was convicted and died in prison, answering perhaps then only to God for the evil he had done. Lazarus's soul would eventually mend, though it would take years. With enough time, with enough caring therapy, and most especially, with the unconditional love of his wife, Lazarus reclaimed his life and his soul. He found peace in his heart, he found understanding from his wife, but from his church he found just the cold, sterile indifference of an institution that wished he would just go away.

As I sat there that day listening not just with my ears but also with my heart, I came to realize the sheer grace given me. While I had been pondering and praying about how to best communicate the suffering, death, and resurrection of Christ to my parishioners, the paschal mystery was staring me in the face. How could I not have made the connection between the Holy Week and Lazarus's story? How can any of us not see the face of Christ crucified in Lazarus—but also resurrected in him as well? Yes, as the poet said, there is a *certain slant of light* in the long winter's night. And so it was on that day as I sat across from Lazarus that I asked, knowing just what it was to ask, if he would consider sharing his story with my parish, the good people with whom I share my life. Unbelievably, he said yes.

Imagine, if you can, a victim of the priest sex abuse scandal, a survivor, standing in the midst of a stripped and empty sanctuary, save for the crucifix. Imagine a Lazarus standing beneath the crucified Christ. How many times had I preached here and said that it could only be here, at the foot of the cross of Jesus, where true healing could be embraced? How many hundreds of broken hearts and bodies and souls had I anointed in this place? How many hundreds of people had I gathered there to pray? Good Friday is good, not because of the tragic events that transpired long ago, but because of the opportunities and the possibilities that arose from such tragedy. The foot of the cross is where heaven's hope and humanity's wounds meet. However, it was not necessarily Lazarus's wounds that needed binding that night. It was ours. So on that long winter's night Lazarus ever so gently, but ever so courageously, unbound the wrappings of his wounded soul in order to bind ours—to bind my soul and the souls of the good people I feel blessed to serve. By showing us the scars left upon his soul, Lazarus helped us to accept the scars on ours. By shedding his tragic tears, Lazarus helped us to cry. By telling his story, Lazarus helped us make sense of ours. And all the while this wounded healer stood beneath the cross of Jesus.

Good Friday and the Cross of Jesus

It is here at the foot of the cross, perhaps it could only be here, where I now choose to see my priesthood. It is at the foot of the cross where I ponder a seemingly endless winter's night. I invite you to join me in the darkness and silence of this place. In one of the final scenes of Mel Gibson's film *The Passion of the Christ,* a solitary raindrop falls from a dark and stormy sky. For me, this was, and forever will be, the proverbial and always poignant teardrop of God—a teardrop possessing an eternity of grieving. This simple scene washed over me as if it were a line in a poem. And though it has appeared in a few articles and a few sermons, in time it became a prayer in a poem:

> An angel of God descends from the heavens
>   above
>   with wings whispering—and O so gently
>   with such ageless care—
> reaches deep inside humanity's wounded and
>   broken heart
>   and there reclaims heaven's once such sad
>   spent tear.

Mine is a church, and mine is a priesthood, drowning in tears. And yet I cannot help but believe that we are even now being baptized in these very tears. For here, too, there is a certain dying that needs to take place. A certain dying so that a certain rising might be possible.

How different this scene is when compared with the Church Triumphant, which once built the mighty cathedrals of Europe, literal visions of heaven on earth. Or how completely contradictory this notion is when compared with the new and emerging Church Militant, arising again with defiant banners waving. My church, I confess, is just a "Church Grieving," crouched in a deep and sincere humility at the foot of the cross of Jesus. Or at least I believe it should be.

There is yet another voice crying out here in the wilderness, should anyone trouble themselves enough to listen. It is the chant of the auctioneer's cry, selling off the treasures of the church, piece by piece. A once triumphant church is dying bit by bit, diocese after diocese—even my own diocese—weighing the benefits and merits of corporate bankruptcy. And we ask ourselves, just what is the fair market price of justice? Pound for pound, and a pound of flesh? Billions, yes billions, already spent, and perhaps billions yet to go, so we are told. But no matter the money, the true cost of the priest sex abuse scandal will undoubtedly cost us more. In the end, it will inevitably cost us our souls.

We as church need to grieve the death of our illusions, if for no other reason than we might be able to accept and embrace our responsibilities. There is no better place and no more authentic moment to grieve our church than at the foot of the cross of Jesus—here and now. On Good Friday a few years ago I shared with my parishioners an experience I had while on annual retreat. I had escaped the winter, or so I thought, for a precious few days in the Arizona desert. Like countless others before me, I had sought the desert for solace and meaning and purpose in life. I recounted in my homily how early one morning I was "making the stations," as we used to say. The Way of the Cross had been carefully and prayerfully laid out along a path that wound its way through the desert hills. I recalled how I had made the stations countless times before but always as just one of the nameless and faceless people in the crowd. Never was I actually a part of the story but was always a spectator witnessing a spectacle.

But that retreat morning proved to be different. I started out on my pilgrim way with a disposable styrofoam cup filled with instant coffee in my hand, and nothing really to speak of in my heart. Somewhere along the way, I can't exactly remember just where, I quite inadvertently inserted myself into the story. I vividly remember that by the eleventh station (*Jesus is nailed to the cross*) I had both lost and found myself all in the same moment. I found myself completely absorbed in the story, and every time I looked for the face of Jesus, I found only mine. Suddenly I found myself on my knees, my face buried in my hands, smeared with tears mixed with dust. Somehow, and I am not exactly sure how, I stumbled and fumbled along my way to the top of a nearby hill, to the final and fateful station, station fourteen (*Jesus is buried*). It was here that I chose to bury my old life that I might embrace whatever my life might then become.

This is the story that I shared with my parish on the fearful night we call "good." I looked intently into their faces and told them that if I am to be a priest, this, and really only this, would be my fate: my life for his, my church for his—to be here, at the foot of the cross of Jesus, when all the others have walked away. No fame, no glory, save in the cross alone. A faith rendered into ruin, a church reduced to rubble, and an abandoned people left to wander, wounded and bleeding from the scandal. And heaven asks, *"Will you stay and care for my people?"* All I can respond is, *"Lord, where would I go? You alone have the words of eternal life"* (see John 6:68).

Good Friday is almost always a night full of tears, and our grieving nearly drowns us. But it is important to remember that our tears of mourning will one day be transformed from grieving into grace. I really don't think I could appreciate Good Friday, I don't believe it will be possible to survive this scandal; I don't believe I could even now be a priest, had it not been for Lazarus sharing his story earlier as he stood under the cross of Jesus. It was in listening to the story of Lazarus that I came to believe, came to hear that "the cries of those victimized at the hands of those who would pretend to be Christ are in fact the cries of Christ, and therefore, the cries of the modern priesthood."

Chapter Three

Winter's Healing Wounds

Robert Frost, the poet whose name is nearly synonymous with winter itself, once penned this rhyme:

> The way a crow
> Shook down on me
> The dust of snow
> From a hemlock tree
>
> Has given my heart
> A change of mood
> And saved some part
> Of a day I had rued.[16]

Snow has been that one aspect of winter, so symbolic, that has thus far escaped our winter's night. And yet, snow really is not as simple as it first appears, or as it appears to so effortlessly fall from the sky. The native peoples of South Western Alaska, the Yup'ik, possess dozens of different words for snow. This is perhaps unsurprising, since snow, after all, makes up a good part of their world and an even bigger part of their daily lives.

But the one Yup'ik word for snow that strikes me most, the one word that causes my mind and soul to stop and to ponder, is *qanisquinineq*—literally, "the snow floating upon the water."

Listening to and learning from the cries of those my church has harmed is nothing if not a delicate venture, much like the snow that ever so precariously floats upon the water. We need to approach this venture with the utmost care and understanding, seeing it as an opportunity for our priesthood, my priesthood, to become more authentic, more actualized within the paschal mystery of Jesus Christ. It might be that it is not really so much the victims' pain shaming our pain as it is their pain shaping or even reshaping our pain.

It has been more than thirty years since Henri Nouwen first graced us with the notion of the "wounded healer." Possibly enough time has passed and enough things have transpired for us to take yet another look through this window into the soul of our priesthood. But perhaps it is not enough just to look. Maybe what is really needed is to actually live and minister through this crisis as wounded healers. For Nouwen, the minister or priest "is called to be a wounded healer . . . who must look after his own wounds but at the same time be prepared to heal the wounds of others."[17] The wounded healer, I sincerely feel, is both poet and prophet for us in our time of need. As poet, the wounded healer fashions and forms his words from deep within his broken heart and wounded experience, still deeper within his grieving soul. Here he gives voice to the hopes and dreams of those he is called to serve. As prophet, the wounded healer looks deep into the human heart and dares to speak to the seriousness of the situation, acknowledging his own pain and suffering, even as he acknowledges that of others. From this broken place he courageously speaks, not with an anxious fear but with a strong and gentle faith. Beyond being both poet and prophet, the wounded healer is also, and most especially, a caretaker, a caregiver, a shepherd of souls, in short—a "Pastor." And it is precisely this notion, this idea, that I fear we have lost sight of in the midst of this scandal and crisis.

Nouwen names his pain as loneliness—loneliness in both a personal and professional sense. I believe that our pain, my pain, as a priest is not really so much a matter of loneliness, though loneliness is nearly always present. Rather, our pain is quite simply the loss of our identity, albeit a mythical identity at that. I contend that what is needed is to strip away all the theological jargon, all the talk of such things as ontological changes (referring to the notion that the very essence and meaning of a priest's being and personhood—of who he is and forever will be—is irrevocably changed upon the day of his priestly ordination). And while I might not necessarily want to deny all of this notion, I do see the need to look beyond it, perhaps even beneath it, when it serves only to prevent us from hearing the cries of those we have so harmed, or prevents us from feeling their pain. Only then will we truly get at the heart of the matter. Long before we ever dreamed of, or feared, our present-day scandal, Nouwen wrote:

> The minister . . . is called to recognize the sufferings of his time in his own heart and make that recognition the starting point of his service. . . . [H]is service will not be perceived as authentic unless it comes from a heart wounded by the suffering about which he speaks. Thus nothing can be written about ministry without a deeper understanding of the ways in which the minister . . . can make his own wounds available as a source of healing. [18]

If ever we hope to make our way through this, our long winter's night, I believe it will be only when we priests acknowledge our wounds, confess our sins, and ask for forgiveness from those we have so grievously harmed. Only with a true contrition will we be able to reclaim our authenticity. No, the suffering wounds of the true victims of our abuse need not necessarily shame our pain; they could actually transform it, especially as we offer ourselves as wounded healers in these most scandalous of times. For what are these wounds if they are not the shame and guilt of our brother priests and of our church as well? And these, the scarlet letters we wear upon our hearts, could they not in fact become the stripes Christ bore upon his back? We sympathize; we identify with Christ as he stumbled and fell beneath the weight of his cross. Could not, then, sharing the shame of our brother priests, our guilt by association, elicit the same? Would Christ do any less? What was it that St. Paul preached?

> *For our sake [God] made him [Christ] to be sin, who did not know sin, so that we might become the righteousness of God in him.* (2 Corinthians 5:21)

If we hope to live out our priesthood in authenticity and integrity, it will be when we accept the whole of it, especially the cross. After all, isn't this the very nature of the Christ we have chosen to follow? Isn't this the very image of Christ that we have chosen to portray? And isn't this the very same Christ as foretold in the prophecy of Isaiah?

> *He was spurned and avoided by men,*
>   *a man of suffering, accustomed to infirmity,*
> *One of those from whom men hide their faces,*
>   *spurned, and we held him in no esteem.*
> *Yet it was our infirmities that he bore,*
>   *our sufferings that he endured,*
> *While we thought of him as stricken,*
>   *as one smitten by God and afflicted.*
> *But he was pierced for our offenses,*
>   *crushed for our sins,*

Upon him was the chastisement that makes us whole,
   by his stripes we were healed.
We had all gone astray like sheep,
   each following his own way;
But the LORD laid upon him
   the guilt of us all.
Though he was harshly treated, he submitted
   and opened not his mouth;
Like a lamb led to the slaughter
   or a sheep before the shearers,
   he was silent and opened not his mouth.
Oppressed and condemned, he was taken away,
   and who would have thought any more of his destiny?
When he was cut off from the land of the living,
   and smitten for the sin of his people,
A grave was assigned him among the wicked
   and a burial place with evildoers,
Though he had done no wrong. (Isaiah 53:3-9)

Just imagine if this particular passage were actually proclaimed at the ordination of a priest. Yet I cannot think of a better creedal statement for our priesthood today. But honestly though, it does not feel much like springtime, does it?

The snows of winter disguise a good many things, some beautiful, some not. While I might not wholly agree with Martin Luther's concept of the justified man being like a snow-covered dunghill (justification meaning that by faith alone we are to appear before

God), I do confess to God's amazing grace as it blankets and covers our sinfulness and our broken human natures. I reflected on this analogy in the spring of 2006, somewhere near the time of break-up, when I was again invited to write a column for our local paper:

> As the long winter's bleakness finally and mercifully releases its icy grip, and our world is once again reborn into spring, we rediscover all sorts of things hidden under the snow. Some of what is revealed is magical and mystical: the trees beginning to bud and the flowers preparing to bloom. Some of it is not so magical but still perhaps a bit mystical: trash strewn along the roadsides—the remnants of a throw-away society. An old abandoned car, long since forgotten under the cover of snow, but never really gone. . . . But look beyond the rust and decay, look beyond what the world calls ugly, old, and useless, and see. Truly see it. It really is, if you think about it, a mystical thing. Some might dare call it beautiful. Oh, the places it's been, and the people it's met, and the experiences it's had and shared. Still, from deep within it echoes the laughter of good times. Upon its weary frame the stains of the tears from times perhaps not so good. Once the source of so much pride and admiration, now just the object of disdain and embarrassment.[19]

Yes, the winter's snows veil a multitude of things, even the opportunities and the possibilities that live and breathe from deep within our wounded and broken selves, and even our priesthood. Life has forever changed for us priests; there is no denying it. When we freely choose to embrace this winter's night, we choose then to embrace our own woundedness, and this we do in order that we might become healers—wounded healers:

> For a deep understanding of his own pain makes it possible for him to convert his weakness into strength and to offer his own experience as a source of healing to those who are often lost in the darkness of their own misunderstood sufferings. This is a very hard call, because for a minister (priest) who is committed to forming a community of faith, loneliness is a very painful wound which is easily subject to denial and neglect. But once the pain is accepted and understood, a denial is no longer necessary, and ministry can become a healing service. [20]

After all, isn't this what it means to be a pastor in a church that is grieving? A priest in a parish that is weeping?

Winter possesses its own rare form of healing and rejuvenation. Each year, in the last few precious days of September when the snows have begun to fall and to cover the ground, we celebrate a Mass of Healing in our parish. I welcome the parishioners by simply stating the reason we gather:

> We come to this place because we are broken. We
> come to this place because we are wounded. We
> come to this place because we hurt and are in
> pain. We come to this place because we do not
> know where else to go, and perhaps because there
> is no other place we can go. We come to the foot
> of the cross of Jesus because it is here, and could
> only be here, where faith is believed and healing
> is hoped. Standing here, kneeling here, falling
> here, we are not despairing, we are not defeated.
> Yes, ours is a world weeping, ours is a church
> grieving, ours is a heart breaking, for what could
> be, for what should be, for what was meant to be.
> And so we have come here weeping, grieving,
> and bleeding, all in the hope of healing.

> So, my sisters and brothers, I invite you to come
> here with all your suffering and all your sorrow.
> Come with all your tears and all your trials. Come
> with all your hope and all your dreams. Come
> carefully, and gently place them all upon this altar
> of sacrifice, this table of love. Come and offer
> them like the bread that is blessed and broken,
> broken and blessed, for this is the holy exchange
> of gifts, and really it is all that we have to offer.

While this sacrifice, this holy exchange of gifts, has always been a part of my priesthood, only now as a pastor have I come to appreciate its true meaning and the fullness of its demands. As a pastor I feel the need to share my brokenness, my woundedness. Recently, as I looked out on the faces of those I feel so blessed to serve, I heard myself saying:

> To be church is to acknowledge and to embrace the fact that your crosses are mine, and mine are yours. You share in mine, I share in yours, and together we share in Christ's. Yes, there is sadness, but there is also joy. Yes, there is grieving, but there is also grace. Yes, there is dying, but there is also rising.

Nouwen puts it like this:

> No minister can save anyone. He can only offer himself as a guide to a fearful people. Yet, paradoxically, it is precisely in this guidance that the first steps of hope become visible. This is so because a shared pain is no longer paralyzing but mobilizing, when understood as a way to liberation. When we become aware that we do not have to escape our pains, but that we can mobilize them into a common search for life, those very pains are transformed from expressions of despair into signs of hope.[21]

In the parish church I call home, at the foot of the cross of Jesus, the same cross where a survivor once stood unwrapping his pain and his healing, there stands an altar. It is not much to look at, just a simple table made of oak and cedar, but upon it I believe miracles do happen. With all the renewed emphasis and effort to reclaim and defend the real presence of Christ in the Eucharist, I wonder if perhaps it would be best if we priests began by first reclaiming the Eucharist's true and full meaning for ourselves and for our priesthood. In a world filled with "what ifs," what if we priests actually lived out the mysteries we preach and pray? And rather than complaining and lamenting about all those Catholics who choose not to believe, what if we priests started to preach and to pray from our broken hearts and wounded places, still deeper, from within our grieving souls? What if, with some poetic license understood (which is to say, exchanging "wheat" for "oat"), we dared to live out the words of the Welsh poet Dylan Thomas:

This Bread I Break

This Bread I break was once the oat,
This wine upon a foreign tree
Plunged in its fruit;
Man in the day or wind at night
Laid the crops low, broke the grape's joy.

Once in this wine the summer blood
Knocked in the flesh that decked the vine,
Once in this bread
The oat was merry in the wind;
Man broke the sun, pulled the wind down.

> This flesh you break, this blood you let
> Makes desolation in the vein,
> Were oat and grape
> Born of the sensual root and sap;
> My wine you drink, my bread you snap.[22]

At the Mass of the Lord's Supper on Holy Thursday, the year the scandal broke, and broke yet again (2002), I carefully and deliberately chose these words:

> We stand witness to the transforming power of our God. Like the bread blessed and broken—now his own flesh—so our brokenness is transformed into wholeness. And like the cup blessed and shared—now his own blood—so our woundedness is transformed into holiness. For nothing is impossible for God. In great humility, and even greater hope, we too testify to the wonders of God's transforming love.

The table, the altar, and even the cross are not Christ's alone, but they are ours as well. And really, what do we have to offer but ourselves, our broken selves? Standing in the shadow of Christ's cross, standing alongside the hurting and holy people of God, standing here at this table is where faith is believed and healing is hoped. This is what I choose to believe.

What would a healing priesthood look like, and more important, what would it have to offer a grieving church? As a sign and symbol of healing Nouwen offers us the virtue of hospitality, "the virtue which allows us to break through the narrowness of our own fears and to open our house to the stranger, with the intuition that salvation comes to us in the form of a tired traveler."[23] Making our way through this long winter's night of the sexual abuse crises, we most urgently need the gift of hospitality. But we also need humility—not humility that is meek and mealy but humility that leads to hope. As a poet and preacher, words fascinate me, especially words like *humility*. Humility shares its common root with both *humus* and *humanity*. The humility of which I speak is born of the earth itself, from the very soil (or humus) from whence we came, from which we were fashioned and formed. It is inherent to our humanity; it is part and parcel of who we are, as from the first day of our creation. This humility defines who we are, especially in relationship to our creator. Elie Wiesel, in his book *The Messengers of God*, shares a wonderful story of the creation of Adam: "In the beginning, man is alone. Alone as God is alone. As he opens his eyes he does not ask, Who am I? He asks, Who are You? In the beginning, man oriented himself solely in relation to God—and all creation defined itself in relation to man."[24]

Being justified before God is perhaps not so much being covered with the white fluffy snow (or in the Yup'ik language, *muruaneq*, meaning "the deep snow that covers the ground") of God's redeeming grace. For

this is the snow, the grace, that conceals instead of reveals us in all our humanity before our God. This grace
is, instead, standing in the acknowledgment of the
"Other"—always the Other—who from the beginning
stands before us. As devastating as the fall from paradise
was, it does not negate the very nature of who God is
and who we are. The virtue of a true humility dares to
lay claim to the central existential reality that God is
God, and we are those who dare to open our eyes and
see God. Moreover, a true humility beckons us to see
even more, to open our eyes even wider, our hearts
wider still, all in the longing belief that what was once
lost can be found, that what was once fallen can be
raised, and that what was once broken can be mended.

A wounded, but healing, priesthood clings to a
humble deity, a more human Christ. While never denying Christ's divinity, our broken but blessed priesthood
grabs hold of a Savior who is ever present within our
sufferings. I fear, though, that we are losing sight of the
very humanity of the incarnate Word, the Logos who is
flesh and blood. This is the God who walked among us,
the God who even now longs to bind our wounds and
dry our tears. This is the God who has become nearly a
stranger among us. Opening our eyes of faith, in the
midst of this crisis of faith, perhaps as if for the very
first time, we priests might well ask, like Adam before
us: "Who are you? You in whose image we are made
and in whose name we pray?" This is the Christ who,

though he may not take away our suffering or our pain, transforms that suffering and gives it new purpose and meaning. As Nouwen writes: "The awareness of loneliness might be a gift we must protect and guard, because our loneliness reveals to us an inner emptiness that can be destructive when misunderstood, but filled with promise for him who can tolerate its sweet pain."[25]

Perhaps this is the scar left upon my soul, this the *qanisquinineq*, the snow that floats on the waters.

Healing, be it physical or spiritual, is at its core relational. It is not intended to be experienced in desolate isolation. This may be why Nouwen names his pain, and the pain of the wounded healer, as loneliness. The wounded healer needs community, the community entrusted and given to him and, just as important, him to them. If ever we hope to make sense of our pain as priests, if ever we hope to make our way through our self-inflicted crucifixion, if ever we allow ourselves to be transformed by it, it will be when we place ourselves within the heart and soul of the Christian community, a community that for Nouwen is "a healing community not because wounds are cured and pains are alleviated, but because wounds and pains become openings or occasion for a new vision."[26] It is precisely this new vision that captivates my imagination, even as it haunts my soul. It's a completely new way of seeing and being church together, and this is what I have dared to see outside my window.

The Story of Simon

I first met Simon (a pseudonym befitting someone who carries another's cross) one winter's day when I was visiting at a local hospital. Simon was new to our faith, a neophyte, having been received into the Catholic Church just a few years earlier. He had gone to the hospital for what was supposed to be a relatively minor procedure. But things went terribly wrong, with one complication leading to another, and then to yet another. All told, an overnight visit turned into a six-month stay.

But the day finally came for Simon to go home, even though this meant being confined to a hospital bed that had been set up in the living room of the small house he shared with his wife. Simon suffered chronic pain from which there promised to be little or no relief. Moreover, he was told he would have to live with this pain for the rest of his life. He was only fifty-two.

After letting Simon get settled in at home, I went to visit a few days later. I pulled up a chair next to his bed, held his hand, looked into his eyes, and asked, "How are you doing?"

"I hurt," he answered.

"Yes, I know."

Simon then said something that haunts my soul— and the soul of my priesthood—even to this day. He looked intently at me and said, "The only way I can make peace with this pain, the only way I can make any sense of it, is to believe that there is someone out there somewhere who cannot carry it. And so I need to do it for them." He continued, "I don't like it much, but I'll do it."

I recall sitting there dumbfounded. Here I was, someone schooled in all the spiritual disciplines, but lying before me was a man who possessed true and authentic holiness. Though a neophyte and a novice in the spiritual life, confined to bed and plagued with pain, Simon had been given the rare and precious gift of redemptive suffering. I soon realized, perhaps for the first time in my life, that I was looking into the very eyes and heart of Christ, who in turn—in truth—was holding my hands, not me, his.

Snow is not as simple as it first appears, as it seems to fall effortlessly from the sky. But it has, I confess, *"saved some part of a day I had rued."* Be this the Dark Night of my soul or the "Great White Silence" of my life, I believe there is something of real value and purpose in my long winter's night—not just for me alone, not just for priests, but, indeed for our whole church. This is without doubt an unfamiliar landscape for priests, for now we stand stripped before our God, grieving over what could be, what should be, what was meant to be. Mine is neither a Church Triumphant nor a Church Militant. It is just a Church Grieving.

Chapter Four

Spending Our Winter's Night Grieving

The psalmist, who I suspect is somewhat of both a poet and a prophet, begins his woeful lament:

> *By the rivers of Babylon*
> *   we sat mourning and weeping*
> *   when we remembered Zion.*
> *On the poplars of that land*
> *   we hung up our harps.*
> *There our captors asked us*
> *   for the words of a song;*
> *Our tormentors, for a joyful song:*
> *   "Sing for us a song of Zion!"*
> *But how could we sing a song of the* LORD
> *   in a foreign land?* (Psalm 137:1-4)

It has been said that following the death of his wife, Mary, in 1861 the poet Henry Wadsworth Longfellow spent his winter grieving. It may be tempting for us to do the same, fearing ourselves to be wrapped in a blanket of such sorrow. In the north there always seems that moment, that most grievous moment, when desperation settles in, and it feels as though winter will never end. When all the while the world seems helplessly, hopelessly trapped beneath the ice and the snow. When we too sit mourning by the frozen waters of what used to be, weeping as we remember how things ought to be.

What is this Church Grieving of which I dare to speak? To some it must seem a scandal. To others, sheer heresy, and to still others, merely factitious make believe. But to those who would risk seeing out the window from which I look, the Church Grieving is no myth and no mystery. As a priest, a poet, a preacher, and a pastor, how can I not see the tear-stained faces that stare at me on any given Sunday morning, their hearts broken, their dreams shattered? And what of the countless many who have simply faded away, who quietly slipped away from their pews, choosing instead to grieve alone. The seventeenth-century English poet William Strode, in a poem titled "On a Gentlewoman Walking in the Snow," wrote:

> And overcome with whiteness there
> For greife it thaw'd into a teare,
> Thence falling on her garment's hem
> For greife it freez'd into a gem. [27]

Grieving is important, crucially important, if we are ever going to dream again.

Shortly before her own passing in 2004 Elisabeth Kübler-Ross cowrote a book with David Kessler titled *On Grief and Grieving: Finding the Meaning of Grief Through the Five Stages of Loss.* She, who had already given so much to help us understand and accept our own dying, blessed and graced us with this one final parting gift. The gift helped us learn not only to accept our dying but to accept our mourning as well. In the afterword of the book she wrote: "Grief transforms the broken, wounded soul, a soul that no longer wants to get up in the morning, a soul that can find no reason for living, a soul that has suffered an unbelievable loss. Grief alone has the power to heal."[28]

What, then, is the grief we grieve if not the loss of our innocence and mythical identity? And yet by this same grief it became possible to be bound to the true victims of this scandal, to those whose pain shames and shapes our very own. Our loss, as theirs, points not just to what once was but, more important, to what could have been.

In the years I have been blessed to be a pastor I have come to appreciate, and dare to say reverence, not just the particular souls of people and believers but the soul of the parish that I serve. And if indeed this can be said of a parish, could it not be said of the whole body of believers and of the Roman Catholic Church? Is there a *corporate soul* to our church? A soul that grieves even as it pleads? I believe, I have to believe, that there must be. For this is the church I both know and serve. Yes, mine is a Church Grieving, but no less a Church Believing.

Kübler-Ross and Kessler invite us upon a familiar journey, something buried deep within us—the Five Stages of Loss. They caution us, however, that though our grief is often a shared journey, it is also uniquely individual:

> The five stages—denial, anger, bargaining, depression, and acceptance—are part of the framework that makes up our learning to live with the one we lost. They are tools to help us frame and identify what we may be feeling. But they are not stops on some linear timeline in grief. Not everyone goes through all of them, or goes in a prescribed order. [29]

All this gives me great comfort and solace, even as it challenges me to a greater understanding of my church's grieving. And, with this better understood, I wonder if we might not turn to these five stages in order to better understand this crisis of our corporate soul.

Denial—Believing the Unbelievable

Throughout this book, I have accused the church, my church, of underestimating the seriousness of the situation. Perhaps I need further to confess to the harshness of my judgment. I have come to better understand through Kübler-Ross and Kessler that even the "Institutional Denial" can be a part of our grieving process and that this denial itself should not be denied. This is not to say that I necessarily accept it, or that I embrace it, but only that I can at least begin to possibly understand it. Denial serves a vital and necessary purpose in the process of grieving: "There is a grace in denial. It is nature's way of letting in only as much as we can handle. . . . We can't believe what has happened because we actually can't believe what has happened."[30] After all, who could believe that a priest, acting in the person of Christ, could actually commit such crimes, such sins? Or even that a church, claiming to possess Revealed Truth, could so intentionally deceive and conceal such depravities? Denial might indeed serve a necessary purpose, but only for a time. It allows us to continue to function, even if minimally so, all the while our lives and our souls are rent apart by both the tragedy and the trauma of our situation.

The problem, however, arises when the church is properly called to respond in a prophetic and pastoral manner but cannot and will not do so. We don't respond because we can't believe. We don't believe these things actually happened. But they did, and probably still are. Or, sadder yet, we attempt to rationalize and minimize these tragic events and sinful actions by saying that if indeed they did occur, they were not nearly as bad as people have made them out to be. How often we hear it said that it was all the fault of just a few bad priests, a few bad apples; it should not reflect on the whole of the church or the good work that the church has done. But it does.

How many times have we heard from both press and pulpit that it was a statistically insignificant percentage of priests who have actually offended? No higher oc-currence than in the rest of society, and in fact probably lower. As if this somehow excuses my church caught in scandal. In chapter 1, I alluded to the first few flirting frosts of winter, which I said are easily enough dis-missed from our memories when the sun rises and be-gins to warm our faces. Our denial of our crisis might be understandable, perhaps even necessary, at the be-ginning. But how can we forget the hard, killing frost that fully awakens us to the existential reality of our long winter's night? No, there is no denying the com-ing winter. And there is no denying that these sad and sordid events did actually happen, and are probably happening still.

Anger—Seething from Without and from Within

As a parish priest ministering within a grieving church, I cannot help but be dismayed by the anger and bitterness that so often surround me in my Church. In the Acts of the Apostles we are reminded that in the early church "the community of believers was of one heart and mind" (Acts 4:32). But such is not necessarily the case for the Roman Catholic Church as it enters the twenty-first century. Ours is a church increasingly divided, a church fraught with anger both from without and from within. Why? Why are we so angry? We are angry, I believe, because we are afraid, and it is to our fear, not our faith, that we have chosen to turn. We are afraid we have lost something, something important to us. We are afraid that we have lost who and what we were, or thought we were.

Once upon a time, as all good stories begin, it used to be so very easy, so very clear. We once painstakingly defined the Catholic Church as over and against something—over and against society, over and against the world—and we still do today. We rail against modernism, secularism, relativism, and the many other *"isms"* that plague our scrupulous souls. We believe ourselves to be above such things, inherently different from such things, and strangely "set apart" from such things. We believe our church is to be not of this world but transcendent and beyond this world. For well over two thousand years we tenaciously clung to the notion that we as the Catholic Church, and we alone, held the moral high ground. Some still cling to such an illusion. But how, I wonder, can we continue to do so when our sins, the sins of our church, are splashed and spilled all over the front pages for all the world to see?

Truly, it has become increasingly more difficult to maintain our illusions, or cling to our reputations, or even defend our good name. Kübler-Ross and Kessler remind us: "underneath anger is pain, your pain."[31] I sincerely believe it is our pain that we fear and our fear we express in all our anger. As we now struggle to see our true selves, should we but dare to see ourselves in the midst and middle, in the mire and muck of this scandal, I can at least begin to understand my church's anger, my church's fear, and my church's pain. Though I would like to think of our anger as the righteous anger of an Old Testament prophet, I fear it is instead just the sad whimpering of our fears.

Listen, then, to the winter winds wailing, seemingly coming out of nowhere, but in truth echoing from deep within our grieving, wounded, and weeping souls.

Bargaining—Hearing the Auctioneer's Singsong Cry

What are we to make of the church's multimillion-dollar settlements and Chapter 11 corporate bankruptcies? And what, pray tell, is the true cost of justice? What will it cost us to buy back our good name? What is the bottom line? I must grieve as I watch my church haggle like some marketplace vendor. Arguing over the price of what? I cannot believe it is the price of justice, even for all our talk of justice. I cannot believe it is about healing either, even for all of the hope of healing.

What it seems to be about is the resolution or the determination of the fair market price for an innocence stolen, a childhood denied, and a church shamed. And sad to say, this is the bottom line of it all. Perhaps the only real question that remains is this: just how cheaply can we get through all of it?

I suspect I have shown a bit of my own bargaining, my own grieving, when I wrote of a world filled with "what ifs"—What if the church, my church, had actually practiced what she preached? What if we as a church had confessed our sins and asked and pleaded for forgiveness? What if . . . ? We only have to imagine how things might be different today. "The 'if onlys' and 'what ifs,'" according to Kübler-Ross and Kessler, "cause us to find fault with ourselves and what we might think we could have done differently. We may even bargain with the pain. We will do anything not to feel the pain of loss. We remain in the past, trying to negotiate our way out of the hurt."[32]

The truth of the matter is, for all our noble words and all our feeble efforts, we really just want to be done with it. We just want to put all of this mess behind us and lock it up in some long-forgotten distant past. We so desperately want to believe Bishop Gregory's words: "the terrible history recorded here is history." And so we negotiate, we quibble and we quarrel, and we try to bargain our way out of our grieving and our pain. Thus I am left to wonder if perchance it is here in the midst of all our bargaining that all the talk of the so-called new springtime originates. All the while our true intentions continue to languish in winter, covered by the concealing snow.

* * * * * *

As I write of these things in the long winter of 2008 I sincerely believe that the church is caught somewhere here, between the stages of *bargaining* and *depression,* and still very far indeed from a day of *acceptance.* Furthermore, I contend that many in the church are still mired in *denial,* while others are quite literally seized by their *anger,* all the while the leadership of our church persists in their attempts to *bargain* our way out of all this—hoping and praying it will just be over soon, praying that "this history will be history." But dark is the night, and darker still the soul that weeps as it grieves and dies.

* * * * * *

Depression—The Dark Night Presses in and All Around

> I believe there is a profound sense of sadness, a shared melancholy, a certain malaise in the priesthood of today. It runs far deeper and is far more serious than a simple moral problem of the corporate church. It is the depression that we all fear but will never dare to speak. [33]

It seems a lifetime ago that I gave voice to these thoughts about the priesthood. And if this could be said of the priesthood, could it not also be said of the whole church? I believe there is a certain sadness in our church today, all the talk of a new springtime notwithstanding. But unlike the wailing winds of our anger, this sadness, this depression, has become nearly lost in all the confusion. We fear this depression, and so we distract ourselves with elaborate ceremonies, choosing instead to focus our attention on former days of glory. Yet lying just beneath the surface of all the pomp and circumstance cries a most profound sense of loss. Again, Kübler-Ross and Kessler help us understand: "When a loss fully settles into your soul, the realization that your loved one didn't get better this time and is not coming back is understandably depressing."[34]

We fear this depression almost as much as we fear our dying. But this is the very time we need to acknowledge it and, what is more, to actually embrace it. For if we ever hope to find our way to a place of acceptance, we first must acknowledge our loss. Kübler-Ross and Kessler suggest an intriguing idea, asking us to "invite your depression to pull up a chair with you in front of the fire, and sit with it, without looking for a way to escape. Allow the sadness and emptiness to cleanse you and help you explore your loss in its entirety."[35]

Our depression really need not be some dark and empty place. It could be, that is, if we allow it to be, a most precious grace. Moreover, a shared grief, a communal depression, though perhaps coming from a wound far deeper, is not nearly so lonely. Nor is the sense of isolation and abandonment so severe. Listen closely to the still, quiet darkness, listen and hear the psalmist cry: *"By the rivers of Babylon we sat mourning and weeping when we remembered Zion."* I ask you to accompany me, and together we can join our voices to the psalmist's sad lament.

Acceptance—Baptized into Heaven's Tears

If, then, it be true and our night is barely half spent, nonetheless I am hopeful that the dawning of a new day, a day of acceptance, might still come and surprise us—though I could only begin to imagine when this might actually be and what it might actually look like. Perhaps, when it is all said and done, our acceptance of this scandal might turn out to be the scar left upon our soul. As much as we hope and pray that it will all just somehow go away, this scar might, like a remnant left over from long ago, remind us of the nightmare that will undoubtedly haunt us for a millennium yet to come. Our church is not a stranger to such scars: the Crusades and the Inquisition are but two others. But they are in some ways different from this scar. During those earlier times, we went astray for what we thought at the time were noble causes of faith. Some joined the Crusades as a pursuit of holiness, while some thought the Inquisition was the pursuit of truth. The sexual abuse crisis, however, arose solely because of our sins and our shame. When, O Lord, will we ever learn?

Truly one of the great paradigms or models of our church is the sincere belief that we are the *Living Body of Christ*. Living though we are, we must never forget what is stored safely in the marrow of our collective Christian memory: that fearful and frightful day when Christ was crucified. Do we dare probe, along with Thomas the doubter (called Didymus), the nail marks in Christ's hands and feet? Or put our hand into his side pierced by the soldier's lance? If indeed we are to be a living reflection of the risen Christ, then the crucified Christ must be our self-portrait too. For it was our sin that brought Christ to the cross, and it is our sin, even this crisis, that keeps Christ there. And though we might not necessarily want to accept it we must, as Kübler-Ross and Kessler forewarn us:

> We learn to live with it. It is the new norm with which we must learn to live. This is where our final healing and adjustments can take a firm hold, despite the fact that healing often looks and feels like an unattainable state.[36]

To heal, in and through our grieving, does not necessarily mean that we will become perfect or flawless, or even infallible. It does, however, suggest that we must grow stronger in our weakness, more convicted in our vulnerability, and maybe, just maybe, more whole and holy in our humanity.

There is a story told about the passing of Moses, a story written by Elie Wiesel in his book *Messengers of God*. I am intrigued by the story and over the years have used it as part of my funeral homily. I use it precisely because it speaks, at least to me, of the shared experience of loss.

> [Moses] began to climb Mt. Nebo. Slowly he entered the cloud waiting for him. He took one step forward and turn around to look at the people following him with their gaze. He took another step forward and turned around to look at the men, the women, and the children who were staying behind. Tears welled up into his eyes, he no longer could see anyone. When he reached the top of mountain, he halted. You have one more minute, God warned him so as not to deprive him of his right to death. And Moses lay down. And God said, Close your eyes. And Moses closed his eyes. And God said, Fold your arms across your chest. And Moses folded his arms across his chest. Then, silently, God kissed his lips. And the soul of Moses found shelter in God's breath and was swept away into eternity.
>
> At the foot of the mountain, shrouded in fog, the children of Israel wept. And all creation wept. And in his sorrow, Joshua forgot three hundred commandments and acquired seven hundred doubts.[37]

Like the children of Israel, we also weep. Yet even in
our grieving we need not abandon our faith. For it is
our faith that gives meaning, even purpose, to our
grieving. It is our faith that moves us beyond our tears,
beyond our fears, and into our healing. Some years ago,
I preached a series of sermons during Holy Week in
which I followed the journey of a tear as it made its
way from Passion (Palm) Sunday to Easter.

Baptized in Heaven's Tears

We enter now into the Promise of Jerusalem
amid shouts of Hosanna—and shouts of cheer.
Our spirits soar . . . and our hearts rejoice . . .
receiving our King. Branches of palm waving in
our hand, our eyes fill with tears of inescapable
joy as the Promise of the Ages passes by, riding
upon a colt. All things seem possible. . . .

We find ourselves sitting at table—as tender tears
wash our feet in humble service, and the eternal
promise is remembered in the Breaking of the
Bread. Like Bread blessed and broken . . . so too
our hearts . . . broken and blessed. We pass over
from meal into garden, stumbling and slumber-
ing as Christ worries and weeps. . . .

We follow—though from afar, for we are afraid.
Struggling along this our trail of tears. Rachael
cries for her children. . . . Heaven's Father weeps
for his son. Oh, that awful hill of Golgotha, awash

in blood, sweat, and tears. Rising upon its crown, and defiantly standing to the original sin—the redeeming cross . . . drenched in humanity's sorrows. And we, we are baptized into heaven's tears. . . .

By the streams of Babylon, we sat and we wept. By the tomb of Jesus we sit and we weep. Our tears mingle with those of heaven. But this is not the end. . . . Our God is a God of the living . . . not of the dead. And so as in the days of Moses, the waters do part . . . earth's from heaven's, death's from life's. Through them we pass, born again in Heaven's Tears. Jesus now lives and dies no more.

A Church Grieving can be a Church Believing, and a Church Believing can become a Church Healing. Praying for the healing of ourselves and for the healing of those we have so grievously harmed, we imitate the wounded healer, Jesus. And drawing from deep within the well of our pain, our sadness, our brokenness, our shame, we nevertheless still choose to believe. The last line in Kübler-Ross and Kessler's book is a final blessing or benediction, given to those who grieve:

That is the Grace of Grief
That is the Miracle of Grief
That is the Gift of Grief[38]

Chapter Five

Winter's Grieving and Weeping Grace

How do you mend a brokenhearted and soul-scarred church? Is it even possible? I believe it is. Were it not, what would be the point of my priesthood or my life, seemingly spent on such a foolish dream? The old adage is that time heals all things. Perhaps, in time, this might prove true. But that does not mean we do nothing here and now. Passivity, even if caused by our paralyzing fear, rarely, if ever, cures anything. But what of prayer?

The shepherds of our church ask us to pray—to pray for healing, healing for victims, healing for ourselves. As a priest, a pastor, and even a poet of sorts, I readily confess to the power of prayer, and I know God's grace can and does heal all wounds. Yet I am just not sure how hiding in some darkened chapel, kneeling before some bejeweled and gilded monstrance, is going to make right what we have made so very wrong. Kneeling thus in humble adoration, we could, and we should, implore the wounded Christ, broken in the bread. But we should do so much more. For long into winter's night have I prayed, pleading to know just what I must do. And still I kneel, praying and waiting . . .

A Healing Priesthood

Given and graced to be wounded healers, we priests need ourselves to be broken. From this broken and fractured place, we need to reach out to others, humbly offering Christ's gracious gift of healing. Isn't this the very heart of the Gospel we have been given to preach? Isn't this the very priesthood we are promised? Returning for a moment to Henri Nouwen's *Wounded Healer*, we discover a lesson in this legend from the Talmud:

> Rabbi Yoshua ben Levi came upon Elijah the prophet while he was standing at the entrance of Rabbi Simeron ben Yohai's cave. . . . He asked Elijah, "When will the Messiah come?" Elijah replied, "Go and ask him yourself."
> "Where is he?"
> "Sitting at the gates of the city."
> "How shall I know him?"
> "He is sitting among the poor covered with wounds. The others unbind all their wounds at the same time and then bind them up again. But he unbinds one at a time and binds it up again, saying to himself 'Perhaps I shall be needed: if so I must always be ready so as not to delay for a moment.'"
>
> (Taken from the tractate Sanhedrin) [39]

No, we must not delay. Instead, we need to be eager to leap up from our place among the beggars and to see to the needs of others. In this simple story, healing is not passive but active. It is a matter of both our hearts and our hands. As something of our hearts, it tugs at us. It stirs up something in us and awakens within us the awareness that something simply must be done. I have often wondered if we as church have lost this awareness, this sense of urgency. Worse yet, we might know it to be true, but nevertheless we choose to ignore it. Maybe it is our fears that paralyze us, or our insecurities that incapacitate us. But it could be our grieving that now stirs us and awakens us, so I hope and pray. The ministry of healing is not simply some option among others listed in a dusty book of ritual; it is at the very heart of our Christian faith. Why else would we worship a crucified yet risen Christ?

Healing as an Affair of Our Hearts

As a matter and an affair of the heart (broken though it may be), the ministry of healing is at the very center of who we are and are called to be. In St. Matthew's Gospel we read: "When Jesus came down from the mountain, great crowds followed him. And then a leper approached, did him homage, and said, 'Lord, if you wish, you can make me clean.' . . . His leprosy was cleansed immediately" (Matthew 8:1-3). Do we truly wish for healing as the leper did. As Jesus did? And if we dare to say yes, then this healing, if indeed it is of God, must be born in our hearts. We must desire it with a passion reminiscent of Christ's own passion. We need to pray, and pray as if we could sweat drops of blood. For really, what are these drops, if not the tears of a wounded but healing priesthood?

There is no use denying the sexual abuse scandal. There is no use pretending we are not moved by it. There is no use trying just to get through and over it. We must live, and we must love, in the very midst of this scandal, even as we embrace it and are ourselves embraced by it. This is the pain and privilege of our priesthood.

What is it that we priests say each day as we arise to pray? "If today you hear his voice, harden not your hearts" (see Psalm 95:7-8). I believe that it is here, most especially here in this broken and fractured place of our hearts, where the voice of the Lord calls out to us, beckons us, and pleads with us to hear those who cry. For a heart not hardened can be broken, broken and shared with others. As we priests break open the Word each day, so should we be broken. As we break bread each day, so should we be broken. Our brokenness need not incapacitate us in ministry, especially when we allow it to be the source and strength of our labors. St. Paul reminds us, "for when I am weak, then I am strong" (2 Corinthians 12:10). A brokenhearted priesthood is a humbler priesthood, a holier priesthood, a priesthood broken and shared with others.

From within this brokenhearted priesthood we ought to take our rightful place within a brokenhearted church. Not separated or set apart, but standing in solidarity with those who weep. Here we draw strength and encouragement from one another. The Church Grieving is not a deserted and desolate wasteland, nor should it ever be seen as a failure. We know, we have often heard it said, that healing comes to the brokenhearted. Jesus himself, broken for others, first began his public ministry by quoting the words of the prophet Isaiah: "The spirit of the Lord GOD is upon me, because the LORD has anointed me; He has sent me to bring glad tidings to the lowly, to heal the brokenhearted" (Isaiah 61:1). Lest we priests ever forget, we were, in fact, anointed for that same mission and ministry. It is time we say yes once again to the vows and promises we pledged—our hearts broken, blessed, and given for others.

Healing as a Work of Our Hands

As a matter and work of our hands, the ministry of healing is nothing if it is not our prayer to God. When at our ordination we knelt before the bishop, and the palms of our hands were laid open and anointed with the sacred chrism, the bishop prayed: "The Father anointed our Lord Jesus Christ through the power of the Holy

Spirit. May Jesus preserve you to sanctify the Christian people and to offer sacrifice to God" (taken from the Rite of Ordination). On that day of our ordination, our hands and our hearts were laid bare—vulnerable, exposed, open, and innocent. So often now, it seems, our hands, perhaps like our hearts, are clenched into an angry fist. Staring into these clenched fists I wonder how we might ever imagine these to be the healing hands of a wounded healer. They simply cannot be. Together, then, with hearts broken and blessed, we priests need to have hands that are anointed and abandoned. Hands always ready to embrace and to be embraced. Hands forever pierced, but never proud. In short, our hands simply must be the hands of Christ. Of all this, the great mystic Teresa of Avila reminds us in prayer:

> Christ has no body on earth but yours,
> no hands but yours,
> no feet but yours.
>
> Yours are the eyes through which is to look out Christ's compassion to the world;
>
> Yours are the feet with which he is to be about doing good;
>
> Yours are the hands with which he is to bless people now.

What kind of hands do we have? Are our hands full of fear and fright, or full of hope and healing? If we are to be healed of our self-inflicted crucifixion, it will be when we are able to open our hands and use them for the work they were intended to do from the day we were anointed.

Throughout this book I often make reference to the crucifix that hangs in our parish church, under which we have so often gathered when we hurt and are in pain. I do so because the crucifix speaks to me. When our parish commissioned a local artist to carve this image, he told me that after much research, he was dismayed to see how Jesus was usually portrayed as emaciated. But he thought of Jesus as a working man, a man of the people. Furthermore, as a working man himself, this artist deliberately chose to give Jesus working man's hands. Looking now at those same hands, I am moved by their size and strength, their longing and their love. It is as if, had they not been permanently nailed and bolted to the cross, they might actually reach out for me and hold me. The work and ministry of healing needs working hands. It needs hands that are not worried about getting broken, or bloody, or bruised. For these are the hands that are truly blessed to be stained, servile, and scarred. And though our hearts should never be callous, perhaps our hands should very well be. And so we pray, "O Lord, *prosper the work of our hands*" (Psalm 90:17).

If Christ has no hands but ours and if ours are the hands through which he blesses, comforts, and heals those who weep, then we have to open our hands. It is through our hands, and not just our hearts, that we are called upon to offer a sacrifice acceptable to the Lord. But what sort of sacrifice? The prophets tell us what is required. Isaiah says:

> Is this the manner of fasting I wish,
>   of keeping a day of penance:
> That a man bow his head like a reed,
>   and lie in sackcloth and ashes?
> Do you call this a fast,
>   a day acceptable to the LORD?
> This, rather, is the fasting that I wish:
>   releasing those bound unjustly,
>   untying the thongs of the yoke; . . .
> Sharing your bread with the hungry,
>   sheltering the oppressed and the homeless;
> Clothing the naked when you see them,
>   and not turning your back on your own.
>
> Then your light shall break forth like the dawn,
>   and your wound shall quickly be healed. (58:5-8)

And Micah reminds us:

> With what shall I come before the LORD,
>   and bow before God most high?
> Shall I come before him with holocausts,
>   with calves a year old?
> Will the LORD be pleased with thousands of rams,
>   with myriad streams of oil?
> Shall I give my first-born for my crime,
>   the fruit of my body for the sin of my soul?

You have been told, O man, what is good,
and what the LORD requires of you:
Only to do right and to love goodness,
and to walk humbly with your God. (Micah 6:6-8)

These prophets speak to us now as they did to the people in their day. They speak to us of the seriousness of our situation, both its urging and its urgency. We need not wait for some word to come down from on high, for it has already been written on our hearts and on our hands. From deep within my own broken heart, I believe it is up to parish priests to begin this ministry of healing. After all, it was among us, from within the priesthood, that this scandal was born. Furthermore, it is vitally important that we do this work and this ministry within the context of our parishes—never set apart but firmly involved in and involving the parishes that continue to sustain and challenge us. I am convinced that our parishes will undoubtedly support us in a work shared, but they will challenge us in a work neglected.

There is an alb (the white robe worn beneath priestly vestments) that hangs from a hook on the back of the sacristy door. To be honest, it has seen better days. I suppose it closely resembles the one who wears it. It is a bit frayed around the edges, in need of some attention, if not actually mending. It is not made from linen or lace. Nevertheless, I believe it to be a holy thing. The stains of my sweat still stubbornly cling to its collar—no matter how hard I scrub. The stains of my own tears, mixed with sacred oils, still cover its front—no matter how hard I confess. When given recently to explain my alb's rather rough and shoddy appearance, I likened it to the frayed and stained coveralls that hung from the back door of my grandfather's farmhouse. He put them on each day as he went out to work in the fields. And so must I. Is the life and calling of a priest all that much different? As a man of the earth and soil, as a man of sweat and labor, my grandfather's life really was not so different from mine as a priest. And hasn't the time come for us priests, given and graced to be wounded healers, to roll up our sleeves and dare to live out the fullness of our callings?

A few years ago I was given the task of training a newly ordained priest. I remember telling him, "Our job is not to have all the answers, nor to solve everyone's problems; but rather ours is to jump in, with both feet, to actually jump into the muck and mire of life itself, and here to walk with others, and offer them hope." I believed it then, and I believe it still. If ever we hope to make our way through this mess, a mess of our own making, it will be when we cease being afraid and resolve to get our hands dirty—hands not just smeared with the sweet-smelling oil of chrism but hands that oh so gently hold the hurting and holy hearts and souls of those we have been blessed and called to serve. Let our prayer, O Lord, be that our hands would be washed by the redeeming tears of those whom we have so grievously harmed. Really, I confess and believe, there can be no other way.

A Healing Church

Given and then graced to be a Church Grieving, we need to accept our tears and our trials. Our healing, both the healing we offer and the healing we receive, must be rooted in our humility and in our humanity, and always—always in the grace of our God. Pope Benedict XVI, in his encyclical letter on hope, *Spe Salvi*, stresses: "It is not by sidestepping or fleeing from suffering that we are healed, but rather by our capacity for accepting it, maturing through it, and finding meaning through union with Christ who suffered with infinite love."[40] To be a healing church we must accept our cross, even if it is a cross of scandal and shame. We must follow Christ, who once carried the scandalous cross of our shame. Christ's own words challenge us, confront us, and convict us: "Whoever wishes to come after me must deny himself, take up his cross, and follow me. For whoever wishes to save his life will lose it, but whoever loses his life for my sake will find it" (Matthew 16:24-25). If we are who we say we are, if we are what we claim to be, if we really are and want to be church, then there is no other way than the way of the cross.

We accept our grieving, we embrace our sorrow, and we are transformed by our afflictions. We willingly accept and embrace acts of sincere and heartfelt contrition and penance. We do so not that others may see but that we ourselves are changed. For when we are changed, and only when we are changed, God's grace and healing will flow freely and unfettered through our hands and our hearts. Only then will we be truly open and available for this work and ministry of healing. And thus the questions remain and beg to be asked: Will we choose to lose our lives, the very lives we thought we once knew, all in the hope and promise that we will find our lives anew? Is this perhaps, as others far more wise and scholarly than I have already dared to ask, a new Reformation? And while these might seem like frightening words for a frightening time, they need not be. If we are honest about it, brutally and completely honest, are we not always in need of reform?

There lives and breathes a particular singular grace in the long winter's night. It's not so much of what used to be as much as it is of what could yet be. Ours is a night filled with possibilities, a night full of opportunities. Beyond the self-imposed limits of our fears, the only real restrictions on what we could yet be are our broken but blessed hearts, and scarred but sacred souls. If we really believe, if we truly profess and confess our faith in the Word Made Flesh, there is no end to what we as church might become. A foolish dream of a foolish dreamer? Perhaps. Nevertheless, this is the hope, the prayer, that haunts my rising in the morning and nearly every thought throughout my long dark winter's night. I don't, and I won't, pretend to have all the answers, and probably would doubt anyone who did. However, what I can do, indeed, what I am called upon to do as a priest, is to jump into the muck and mire of this scandal, into the pain and privilege of this crisis—with both feet and both hands, but especially, with my heart, broken and blessed.

Chapter Six

Scars Heavy upon Our Priesthood

As the snows of winter's grace settle upon our souls so too a new reality has come to settle upon our priesthood. Listen, then, to an ancient legend:

> An aged woman had a camel. It was her only source of income. But then it was stolen. There was a rich man. Among his thirty camels she found her camel. Everyone was amazed. Would a rich man steal a poor woman's only camel? And how was it possible for her to know a certain camel was hers? She insisted it was hers. "But how can you prove it?" "I can prove it," she said. "How?" "Kill her and open her chest. On her heart you will find a scar." The camel was killed and there on her heart was a scar. It could be easily seen. Everyone was astonished. The rich man gave her two camels as a gift. "How," he asked her, "could you know there was a scar on her heart?" "It was simple," she said. "Two years ago the son of the camel was killed by a wolf. The camel was so sad that I knew it must have left a mark on her heart.[41]

And indeed, there is a mark left on our hearts, a scar left on our souls, as we now contemplate our priesthood. And while this mark, this scar, might be born of sin and sadness, it is not to say that it is without meaning, or purpose, or even promise. To be sure, we priests have experienced a loss. We have been hurt, even as we now come to a fuller realization of those whom we have hurt. But it is precisely from this wounded and broken place that we are called to minister. It is from this broken and wounded place that we stutter and stammer, because as of yet we cannot sing—which might explain but does not excuse our silence It is in this place that we have grieved, and are grieving still. Grief washes over us, baptizing us, as we weep for the life we once knew, or thought we once knew. And it is here in this place, in our long winter's night, that we are given to write a new psalm, a new poem for our priesthood.

In the so-called new springtime of our priesthood much is being said about the so-called priestly character. In a recently published book, *Reclaiming Our Priestly Character*, Fr. David Toups asserts:

> Through ordination, priests receive a sacramental character, which indelibly marks their soul. Acknowledging the permanent nature of this character serves to remind priests of their life-long union, commitment, and relationship with Christ and His Church, and that Christ has also entered into a permanent relationship with them.[42]

Vesting to say Mass, now that nearly twenty winters have passed since my ordination, I pause and ask myself what it is that I see when I look into the sacristy mirror. Is it the Roman collar around my neck, faded, torn, and nearly threadbare? No. Is it the once-bright white alb, now so stained with the oil of both gladness and tears, which in the end serves only to cover my faults, my most grievous faults? No. Daring to look ever deeper, to look beyond and beneath the externals of my church and even my priesthood, I am forced to look into my heart, and here to contemplate the indelible mark left on my own soul. It is here in this mirror that I must face the apparent disconnect between what could be, what should be, and what is.

Fr. Toups accurately reflects church teaching of perhaps the last thousand years or so when he insists: "The ontological change occurs so that a man can more radically serve the people with a strength that does not ultimately come from him. He acts *in persona Christi* sacramentally, ministerially, and in fact, at all times."[43] As a priest, my personal struggle is not really so much something sacramental, or even ministerial, as it is something existential. For how can I grab hold of the idea, the notion, the infallible teaching, that upon the sheer act of my ordination, my former self, a soul prolonged and plagued by sin, simply vanishes to be forever replaced by a soul that acts in the person of Christ at all times. Is it even possible to live with this supposed idealized reality? How do I reconcile this teaching with Leon Podles's disturbing image of Satan wearing a Roman collar (see chap. 2)? Thus my dilemma and my church's as well. Can these two realities (the idealized and the actualized), these two mysteries, these two natures live in the same world, pray in the same church, breathe in the same priesthood, beat in the same heart? Maybe, just maybe, this is the sacred but scarred soul of our priesthood, or perhaps just mine.

It matters not how much I might want to look away, for it is this mark left on the soul of my priesthood that stares back at me each morning as I look in the sacristy mirror. There is a temptation to reduce the notion of this indelible mark to some mere theological construct, composed for a perfect world, and possessed by a church claiming to be without fault. And if indeed this is it, if this is all there is to it, then truly I must fear for my priesthood. For mine would certainly be a priesthood doomed to fade into oblivion, evaporate into obscurity, and possibly even perish into irrelevancy. All this as the world, and possibly the kingdom itself, passes us by.

In one of the final scenes of Graham Greene's novel *The Power and the Glory*, the main character, a most unlikely hero, the nameless but nearly famed whiskey priest, stares at his prison-cell wall early on the morning of his execution. His stare transfixes on the wall of his cell, which transforms into a mirror and serves only to reflect back to himself the state of his soul. Here the whiskey priest dares to see, for truly he has no other choice but to see, things not as they could have been but as they truly are:

> When he woke it was dawn. He woke with the huge felling of hope which suddenly and completely left him at the first sight of the prison yard. It was the morning of his death. He crouched on the floor with the empty brandy-flask in his hand trying to remember an Act of Contrition. "O God, I am sorry and beg pardon for all my sins . . . crucified . . . worthy of thy dreadful punishments." He was confused, his mind was on other things: it was not the good death for which one always prayed. He caught sight of his own shadow on the cell wall; it had a look of complete surprise and grotesque unimportance. What a fool he had been to think that he was strong enough to stay when others fled. What an impossible fellow I am, he thought, and how useless. I have done nothing for anybody. I might just as well never have lived. His parents were dead—soon he wouldn't even be a memory—perhaps after all he was not at the moment afraid of damnation—even the fear of pain was in the background. He felt only an immense disappointment because he had to go to God empty-handed, with nothing done at all. It seemed to him, at that moment, that it would have been quite easy to have been a saint. It would only

> have needed a little restraint and a little courage.
> He felt like someone who has missed happiness
> by seconds at an appointed place. He knew now
> that at the end there was only one thing that
> counted—to be a saint.[44]

I believe the whiskey priest was a saint, a saint if only
by his sheer and desperate brokenness and brutal honesty.
I am also confident that the church, my church, would
never find cause for his canonization. Nevertheless, by
his heartfelt act of contrition, no mere rote words of
empty and pious ritual, and by the scar heavy on his
soul, the scar redeemed into the indelible mark of his
priesthood—he was a saint, well, a saint of sorts. Oh, that
this would be true for all of us priests. Yes, "a *truly spiritual
person (a saint) tries less to be holy than to be deeply human.*"
I contend that within this "certain slant of light," this
particular hermeneutic, the whiskey priest was a saint
precisely because he knew that "he had to go to God
empty-handed." He knew the fullness of this reality in
the very depth of his heart. He knew that he could
never deny his own emptiness. He knew all this from the
lived reality of his own broken priesthood. And he was
able to express it without any theological jargon or ontological bargaining. It is good for us to remember that
in the end, we will all have to go to God empty-handed,
saved only by the pierced hands and wounded heart of
Jesus, in whose very priesthood we now cling.

Thus by God's grace the pains of our priesthood, or maybe just mine, need not be shamed by the pain of the victims of clergy sexual abuse as much as they must be reshaped and challenged by their pain. In the end, when all is said and done, I believe it will be their pain (which *is* Christ's pain) and Christ's pain that will become the very privilege of my priesthood.

The quest for a heroic priesthood lies not in being otherworldly, or in being set apart, but in the desire to conform ourselves more closely to Christ, to conform our lives ever more perfectly to the sacred but scarred heart of Jesus. In the "Great White Silence," in the depth of this our long winter's night I have come to hear an almost impossible conversation. It is a most disparaging debate between the so-called Vatican II priests and the John Paul II priests, between those who cling to "Servant Leadership" and those who insist upon a "Cultic Priesthood." I cannot believe this is just some sort of presbyterial generation gap. I do sincerely believe, however, that ours is a priesthood being reshaped, perhaps even reenvisioned, in light of the clergy sex abuse scandal and crisis. As I listen to impassioned pleas, which rarely if ever connect to one another, as I watch the distrusting stares across tables and generations, I am left to wonder if this is really the new springtime. Or is it still winter outside my window? So I ask myself and anyone who might listen whether ours truly is a church militant and triumphant as we claim. Or is ours a church merely breaking and grieving? Is ours a priesthood praised and exalted? Or shamed and defiled? In the introduction of his book *Confronting Power and Sex in the Catholic Church,* Bishop Geoffrey Robinson bares his soul as he confesses to his pain:

> In 1994 I was appointed by the Australian bishops to a position of leadership in responding to revelations of abuse, and for the following nine years I was at the heart of this storm within my country. I felt sick to the stomach at the stories that victims told me, I spent many sleepless nights and I lived at a constantly high level of stress. Those years left an indelible mark on me, for they led me to a sense of profound disillusionment with many things within my church, typified by the manner in which, I was convinced, a number of people, at every level, were seeking to "manage" the problem and make it "go away," rather than truly confront and eradicate it. [45]

Could Bishop Robinson's nine years of sleepless worrisome-wearisome nights, the indelible mark left on his heart, be the same indelible mark of which Fr. Toups writes? Moreover, can these same indelible marks be the wounds that marked the tragic figure of Graham Greene's whiskey priest? And in the end, is this the very scar on my soul, the scars that now mark my priesthood? What else can I believe? I believe that ours is a broken-hearted priesthood, grieving yet ministering—within a broken church, a church with a mark on its heart.

Chapter Seven

Winter's Redeeming Elegy

Deep within the grieving soul of a poet, deeper yet perhaps within the scarred soul of a priest, there live and breathe the wistful words of "Elegy," that sad song, that pleading poem that cries out in the darkness of winter's night. In this our winter's night I am once again reminded of a Theodore Roethke line, "In a dark time, the eye begins to see." In his poem "Elegy" Roethke writes:

Elegy

1

Should every creature be as I have been,
There would be reason for essential sin;
I have myself an inner weight of woe
That God himself can scarcely bear.

2

Each wills his death: I am convinced of that;
You were too lonely for another fate.
I have myself an inner weight of woe
That Christ, securely bound, could bear.

3

Thus I; and should these reasons fly apart,
I know myself, my season, and I know.
I have myself one crumbling skin to show;
God could believe, I am here to fear.

4

What you survived I shall believe: the Heat,
Scars, Tempest, Floods, the Motions of Man's Fate;
I have myself, and bear its weight of woe
That God that God leans down His heart to
  hear.[46]

Mary Jo Bang writes of the purpose of elegy, of the
reason and the role, the need and necessity, of saying
good-bye. In her poem "The Role of Elegy" she
proposes:

What is elegy but the attempt
To rebreathe life
Into what the gone one once was
Before he grew to enormity.[47]

And so if it is true that poets do, in fact, fashion their
words from deep within the human heart and experience, still deeper within the soul, giving voice to our
hopes, our dreams, our fears, our faith—then perhaps
redemption is not necessarily impossible for our
priesthood. We might again "rebreathe life" into what
once was expired. Yes, I suppose ours is a sad story, and
even what some might call a psalm of lament. But

nonetheless it is our story, a story to embrace, to share, and to tell.

The Long Winter's Night

There are moments in these long winter nights when, while reading and praying the poems and prayers found in the back of my well-worn and duct-taped breviary, I feel nearly afflicted by those haunting first lines of Francis Thompson's mystic poem, *The Hound of Heaven*:

> I fled Him, down the nights and down the days;
>   I fled Him, down the arches of the years;
> I fled Him, down the labyrinthine ways
>   O my own mind; and in the midst of tears.

In the midst of countless tears I am often tempted to flee, or maybe just to hide. But I am hopelessly haunted by Thompson's words, words from which I simply cannot flee. Haunted by these very words that are etched, and carved, and engraved upon my soul, and the soul of my priesthood. Peter Maurin, cofounder of the Catholic Worker Movement, composed in a rather simple but forever memorable verse, which he called his *Easy Essays*. I offer my own rather uneasy essays, my restless ruminations.

The Long Winter's Night

In the long loneliness of winter's night
where truth be told, and heaven waits
where poets and prophets dare to speak
a church protests as it weeps

In the frost and snows of winter's night
where victims die, and suffering waits
where innocence and grace no longer live
a church bleeds as it weeps

In the cold and chill of winter's night
where the air is still, and mercy waits
where priests and pastors care and keep
a church struggles as it weeps

In the wind and storm of winter's night
where tempests rage, and justice waits
where sin and shame are clearly seen
a church laments as it weeps

In the dark and shade of winter's night
where souls are scarred, and redemption waits
where wounded healers unwrap their pain
a church repents as it weeps

In the hearts and hands of winter's night
where bread is broken, and gospel waits
where cross and table appear the same
a church sacrifices as it weeps

In the praise and promise of winter's night
where tears are shed, and healing waits

where past and present are abandoned
a church dreams as it weeps

In the hope and prayer of winter's night
where priesthood is forged, and faith awaits
where confessions live in vows not vice
a church ministers as it weeps

In the blessing and beauty of winter's night
where victims heal, and acceptance waits
where grieving changes into grace
a church heals as it weeps

In the long cold darkness of winter's night
where truth be told while heaven waits
where poets and prophets live to tell
a church is reborn as it weeps

Baptized in Ashes and Tears

I imagine the experience of the winter and of the
desert to be the same, somehow born of the same spirit.
For as in the winter, in the desert the soul is laid bare. In
the winter as in the desert, the soul is revealed in such
stark abandonment. It is for this reason that, throughout
time, holy seekers have sought the desert. Seekers who
have sought to know the unknowable in the desert, to
dwell in the wasteland, a place where I believe poets
plead and prophets prepare. Seeing things differently
now, I have begun to wonder if my desert is made not
of sand but of snow. Here, my winter provides the same

spiritual crucible, where eternal truths are imparted and where my heart is ultimately laid bare.

Before I came to realize that winter and the desert just might be the same, I foolishly attempted to escape winter by hiding in the desert. Most every year I try to break the grasp of the long Alaskan winter with a retreat in the Arizona desert. Yet no matter how much I try to flee from myself, from my wounds, from my priesthood, from my church, the harsh reality of winter inevitably follows me into the desert. Likewise, the desert almost always accompanies me back into winter. My desert prayer and fast do not negate my winter's night; they only validate it. So when last I "fled" into the desert I found these words waiting there for me like some sort of perpetual Ash Wednesday:

Baptized in Ashes and Tears

Our faces smeared in sooted ash
and baptized in tears
Rags and rubble of former glory
the smolderings of what once was

Our Triumphant Church rest in ruin
and buried in scandal
Steeple and spire laying in cinders
the folly of what was thought to be

Our Lofty Standard left abandoned
and trampled underfoot

Gilded gold and bejeweled corruption
the Cross of our proud confusion

Our Holy Innocence squandered
and left in sinful shame
Hopes and dreams shattered forever
the cost of our disgrace

Our remnant Church humbled
and given to begin again
Gospel and God unguarded
the gift of a faith renewed

Our faces smeared in sooted ash
and baptized in tears
hearts and souls reborn
the promise of innocence again

Spurning Not the Humble Heart

Listen closely, then, to winter's warning, for there just might be something to hear upon the winds and whispered from the heart. *Edugh nots' ehulnek ts'en*, in the native Koyokon language spoken by the Athabaskan peoples of the Interior of Alaska, is translated "the way we tell or talk about ourselves." What is it that we tell or say about ourselves in these troubled times? The early missionaries used, borrowed, perhaps even plagiarized these very words to explain, even to name, the sacrament of confession or penance. As the clergy sex abuse scandal has come to settle upon our soul here in the north, it is uniquely experienced. Yes, here it is ecclesiastical, to be sure, but much more, it is cultural. In my somewhat limited experience here, I have come to understand and to truly appreciate just how Alaska complicates things. Whether it is the distance or the weather, I cannot really say. Recalling the immortal line from Dickens, we might just say, "It was the best of times, it was the worst of times." In the best of times two very different worlds live side by side. In the best of times these worlds share a mutual respect and understanding. However, in the worst of times, times such as these, these worlds can fall victim to grave misunderstandings and cultural misgivings. In the worst of times, we confront the fact that most, if not all, victims of clergy sexual abuse in my diocese are Native Alaskan, while all the offending priests were white. In the worst of times, things here in Alaska are particularly complicated.

Being a priest in a place such as this calls one to walk with a foot set in two vastly different worlds. Not only to walk but also to speak, to preach and teach, to listen and learn, even to confess across cultural lines and barriers. It was through this awareness that I gathered a group of people, people from both worlds. Together we began to try and find a way for us, as church, to convey our sorrow and our contrition. And to do so in a way that might not just be heard but, more important, be *received*. One of the first realizations we had was that we needed to place this particular scandal within a larger context of other cultural injustices and sins and that whatever we did needed to be as visual as possible, using as few words as absolutely necessary. What follows is a brief, but I hope meaningful, expression of a brokenhearted but truly repentant church. It is just a first step, and a very small step at that, in a very long journey toward true reconciliation and healing.

This prayer service (originally designed as a homily or sermon) uses two primary symbols: The first is a stick, about an inch in diameter and three feet in length. This stick is a remembrance of a native celebration on the Middle Yukon River, an annual commemoration of the dead, simply called "Stick Dance." The second symbol is four Indian blankets. These blankets symbolize not just the burdens of our guilt but also the possibility of our redemption. (Here I give credit to the "Misconduct Prevention Program" developed by The Faith Trust Institute of Seattle, Washington, from which we drew and adapted this service.)

Imagine a small, remote and isolated Native Alaskan village. The depths of winter's night have surrounded and embraced everything in sight. A priest, dressed in simple Roman collar and holding a stick, stands alone in front of a village that has gathered and begins:

> I come before you now only a simple parish
> priest—who I confess—is a sinner. And I come
> before you now to say that I, that we, that all of

us in the church past and present, are deeply
sorry. They say that words are cheap, especially
when they are many and without much meaning. I promise mine will be few, but please know
they are spoken from the heart.

A hundred some years ago, we came to you with
the best of intentions. We came because the fire
of God's love burned in our hearts, so much so,
we wanted to share it with you; but somehow we
lost our way. Maybe it was because we were too
proud. Maybe it was because we were just foolish.
We thought we had something precious to share,
and, yes, I feel we still do. But we were foolish to
think you did not know God. We reached out to
you in faith—and you reached back to us in trust.
We stepped out of the boat—and you helped us
ashore. You helped us, and we took your language,
your culture, your land, and your innocence. You
trusted us—and we broke your trust. . . .

From the midst of a stark and deafening silence, the
priest suddenly and without warning snaps the stick in
two. The sound of the stick breaking echoes throughout the tribal hall. The priest continues:

And so the time has come to say how very, very
sorry we are. . . .

But I believe, I just have to believe, that things
can be made right. For I, indeed for all of us—
together—and all the People of the Promise—

can be remade in the very image and likeness of our God. But only, only if the truth be told. . . .

And so in the words we once learned and I now pray . . .

I confess to Almighty God and to you, my brothers and sisters, that I—that we—that the Catholic Church, the priests and the sisters have sinned. . . .

The priest walks over to a respected and revered elder of the village, drapes over his head the four blankets, one at a time, saying:

We sinned when we took away your language, and forced you to speak only ours . . .

We sinned when we took away your ways and your culture, and demanded that you follow only ours . . .

We sinned when we took away your land, and claimed it as our own . . .

And most especially, we sinned when you trusted us—and when we violated that trust and stole your innocence, the innocence of your children, by our own acts of lust and perversion and abuse. . . .

The elder is now covered, cloaked, and nearly suffocated by these four blankets, blankets that symbolize my church's sins. The priest explains:

So it is that we now live in the darkness of our sin and our shame, foolishly trying to live with the secrecy of our crime. And should we but choose to remain here, trying to keep our secrets, denying our sin, I know that here we will surely suffocate, and here we will surely die. And so I, all of us, plead for God's mercy—and for yours as well. . . .

Removing each blanket, one at a time, the priest says:

We believe God can restore what was lost. God can make whole what once was broken. I promise that I will do all that is in my power to heal the wounds of clergy sexual abuse and restore the innocence that was lost. . . .

We believe God has created the earth, this land, and all that it contains—this land first given to you. We acknowledge and honor your stewardship, and we look to learn from your ways. . . .

We believe God inspired in you a unique and wonderful culture, rich traditions passed down through countless generations. And we would very much like to help you to preserve these ways for your children's children's children. . . .

We believe God was and forever will be praised and glorified by your tongue and in your languages—and though we did not understand, teach us, we pray, now to understand and to speak with wisdom and truth. . . .

Taking the two pieces of the broken stick, the priest refashions them into a cross by tying them together, saying:

> Yes, I know that words are cheap and that actions speak louder than words. But I also know that all things are possible for those who love God. I know and I sincerely believe that like this cross—once something so broken and filled with suffering and pain—our hearts too can be transformed into a symbol that promises life and healing. Healing for me, healing for you, healing for us all. . . .

The priest humbly and sincerely presents this refashioned cross to an elder, a sign and symbol of the hope of reconciliation. The elder, hopefully, accepts it on behalf of the community.

I have been blessed to use this simple service a handful of times, even adapting it for our parish's Lenten communal penance service. The Koyokon tongue translates our word "reconciliation" as Soo-net'aay neenonuhteeyh, meaning "to put it in place nicely again." What if the church itself would put things in place again, go to confession and confess as a sincere and repentant sinner? Consider this confession, just one of many different forms, consider it done with true sincerity of heart. Might it speak not just to the pain of our situation but also to the possibility of healing? Just what might something like this look like in, say, some remote Alaskan village? Daring to think, to dream in sacraments, mine is a church decreed to kneel and to plead. And as in the Gospel of Luke, our posture should be that of the publican—not of the Pharisee. Oh, that we as church were not so proud, that we could beat our breast and cry, "O God, be merciful to me a sinner" (Luke 18:13).

And rather than standing and preaching against the sin of "relativism," might we as church be on our knees questioning our "relevancy"? I wonder if the church, if indeed the very Gospel we preach, is even relevant in the lives of people today. In a world filled with "what ifs"—What if our shepherds would actually abdicate their roles as C.E.O.s and step out from behind their corporate attorneys? What if our shepherds would divest themselves of their brocaded chasubles and towering miters in favor of sackcloth and ashes? What if our shepherds would lead us in, and by, a life of humble penitence and conversion? What if . . . ? Indeed, a poor parish priest is left to wonder. But we need not wait and wonder. If not us, who? If not now, when? If history has taught us anything, it has taught us that change, authentic and meaningful change, usually rises up from below. Like winter's frost, authentic, transformative change rarely, if ever, comes down from above; rather, it rises up from below. I no longer watch and wait for a new springtime to magically appear outside my window; instead, I now know I must look for it within my heart.

And should I dare to look into my heart and soul, I must now begin to ask how relevant my own life is, my priesthood, my church. Tim Giago, an Ogala Lakota who grew up on the Pine Ridge Reservation in South Dakota, begins his tragic book, *Children Left Behind: The Dark Legacy of Indian Mission Boarding Schools*, with this poetic but honest memory:

The Mission School

It stands like a gothic city,
Red bricks and grey concrete,
In the middle of the Dakota plains
On the Pine Ridge Reservation.

The Jesuit Fathers of the Society of Jesus
Built this bastion of Catholicism in the late 1800s
To spread the religion of the righteous.
I stood last summer at the cemetery,
High on a hill above the church,
And looked at the rows of graves
Of the fathers, brothers, and sisters.

So many of them came from Europe
To serve as missionaries in the wilderness,
To save the souls
Of primitive, savage heathens.

We were as alien to them
As they were alien to us.

They smiled in paternal benevolence;
We scowled in fear and distrust.

Perhaps they didn't save our souls.
But did our souls need saving?
Sometimes they found a convert
As we shook our heads, bewildered.

And now they lie in tiny little rows,
Names chiseled in cold granite,
Flickering names, long-forgotten memories
Of a time not so long ago.
When I pass a Catholic church
Sometimes I remember them,
Not always with fondness, I fear.
But I never enter the church.[48]

Snow Floating upon the Water

From deep within my heart I now pray these lines from
Oscar Wilde's poem "The Ballad of Reading Gaol":

Ah! Happy day they who hearts can break
    And peace of pardon win!
How else may man make straight his plan
    And cleanse his soul from Sin?
How else but through a broken heart
    May Lord Christ enter in?[49]

While we might not necessarily want to admit it,
moreover dare to confess it, ours is a church suffering,

and ours is a priesthood breaking. The Gospel I now preach, more often than not, sounds something like this:

> Christ steals his way into a broken heart, a heart full of pain and full of shame. Christ enters in by means of his own broken heart, pierced by our sin and shame. And here, in the very depths of our broken hearts and sin-sick souls, Christ transforms our fears into faith, our brokenness into blessing, and our grieving into grace.

I believe, I just have to believe, there is a certain grace that enters into a broken and breaking heart, especially if we allow the Crucified Christ to enter in. A Christ not glorified—but crucified. After all, isn't this Crucified Christ the very heart and soul of this scandal, this crisis? If ever we hope to make our way through this long dark winter's night it, will be when we freely acknowledge that the sexual abuse crisis is not just some distraction along the way. Rather, it is part and parcel of the journey itself. I cannot believe that the identity of a priest is really such a mystery after all. For as a poet, a priest, but most of all, as a pastor, I now preach lines such as *Broken Hands—Breaking Bread—For Broken and Breaking Hearts.* Moreover, I believe we have actually been blessed, yes, even in this time of crisis, especially in this time of transformation, to write anew the "Sacerdotal Elegy" for our priesthood. I now choose to

read Christ's words of Matthew 16:19 as an invitation
to *bind the wounds of those whose hearts are broken and
loose the chains of those who hearts are held bound.*

Qanisquinineq

(Yup'ik for "snow floating upon the water")

I. neither heights nor depths

floating on life's surface
neither soaring—nor drowning
but caught precipitously suspended
in the awkwardness of the in-between
endlessly pondering my priesthood
as I drift along upon a dream

II. on the wings of an illusion

in a perfect world
a perfect church preaching
ideologies superseding realities
indelible marks of idealized grace
obscuring a more sinister side
as hands lain upon my head

III. chained to a millstone of delusion

pierced for my offense
iconoclastic windows cracking

a starched collar wilts and withers
my priesthood cries as it complains
from the self-inflicted crucifixion
as I dare to break the bread

IV. baptized in the grace of grief

an innocence stolen
my grievous shame reshaping
the sacrifice of the redeemed offered
breaking hearts anew amidst rivers of tears
rewriting a gospel of victim souls
as if this history—is history

V. embracing the place in between

scars etched upon my soul
fragile snows alight on still waters
the priest, poet, prophet, and pastor
precarious both in being—and in grace
consecrating pain into privilege
as water turns into wine

Conclusion

Longing for Spring

Thus it is that I find myself gazing deep from within, deep from without, the window of my own scarred soul. My soul, with its panes, my pains, graced in such delicate design, asking myself—asking anyone who might be listening—*what does it mean to be a priest these days?* I believe that it is only by listening to the still, small voices that echo through our hearts and our souls in times like these, especially in times like these, that we will be able to hear and discern the notion that being a priest simply means being a *wounded healer, tending to—and always with—a grieving church*.

Recently I stumbled upon a most rare and precious gift, the poems of Denise Levertov. Among them, I discovered one that is both a possible and plausible model for my priesthood:

A Cure of Souls

The Pastor
of grief and dreams

guides his flock towards
the next field

with all his care.
He has heard

The bell tolling
but the sheep

are hungry and need
the grass, today and

everyday. Beautiful
his patience, his long

shadow, the rippling
sound of the flock moving

along the valley.[50]

Along with the lamenting psalmist, I too might fear as
if I were walking through some valley of darkness. As a
priest, a poet, and a prophet of sorts, but most especially as a pastor, I must confess that I still grieve over
what could have been, all the while dreaming of what
might yet be. And though I can only begin to image
and envision what this "next field" might bring, I suspect that as a pastor of both grief and dreams, I will
continue to stumble and fumble my way along. No

doubt this journey is complicated, but never compromised, by my grief and my tears.

Moreover, I am quite certain that there will continue to be, as there already are, many truly fine and scholarly works written about the clergy sex abuse crisis and scandal in the Roman Catholic Church. And though I confess I might not look forward to reading them, undoubtedly I will, adding them to the stack already falling over beside my chair. I do not pretend, nor would I ever intend that this book be included in their scholarly company, for such was not the purpose of my writing. Rather, I confess, yet again, that I am but a simple parish priest, no saint and surely no scholar. And this book? Just a glimpse into the heart and soul of a parish priest who is struggling to make sense of a desperate situation. And myself? Perhaps just a parish priest confessed, perhaps even blessed, by the scar left upon my soul.

Speaking to those we have so grievously harmed, to the true victims of this scandal, how could I (how could anyone really) ever even begin to express the depths of my sorrow, my shame? How could I ever hope to be able to restore an innocence lost, a childhood stolen, a spirit raped, and a soul murdered? I cannot. But what I can do, indeed, what we as church simply must do, is risk seeing—in these, our wounded sisters and brothers—the very Christ whom we ourselves have crucified. That is why I rejoiced when in the springtime of 2008, during his first papal visit to the United States, Pope Benedict XVI humbly confessed to his shame and met with a select handful of victims to share in a rare moment of healing. It seemed that someone in my church finally *got it*. It seemed, even if for the briefest of moments, that the winter's snows were finally beginning to melt.

But winter, as we have seen, is not so easily dismissed, nor are the winds of our duplicity so easily excused. For just days after the pope was once again safely tucked inside Vatican walls, a Vatican official was quoted as saying, "The Pope has helped the American Church to close a chapter of shame and sorrow over the faults and grave responsibilities of the past." But, I dare say, no matter how much we might wish, no matter how much we might pray, this chapter of shame and sorrow is a long, long way from being closed. Furthermore, I believe this sad and sordid chapter is really just now being written. It is ordained to be written upon history's pages, composed of a poet's verse and a prophet's curse. This is the story destined to be written upon the sacred texts of broken hearts and shattered souls—a soul perhaps such as mine.

It has been nearly twenty long winters since I first stood nervously trembling at the table, blessing and breaking the bread, daring to proclaim Jesus wounded and weeping in the breaking of the bread. And still do I cry from the midst of my hunger and my pain. It is this mournful cry I choose to hear in the Great White

Silence of this, my Long Winter's Night. And though I readily confess I do not know where, or even what, "the next field" might bring, I know in the depths of my heart and soul that as a priest and as a pastor—a pastor of both grief and dreams—that I simply cannot turn away. Instead, I embrace both the mission and ministry of guiding my flock with care, broken though we both may be. Fr. Toups might indeed claim: "For the priest to be the healer Christ desires him to be, he must first be healed and continually reconciled. The priest is not simply a 'wounded healer'; he is to be a 'healed wounded healer,' turning constantly to the Divine Physician to be mended and made whole."[51] But as a priest in these days of crisis and scandal, pain and privilege, I cannot lay claim to being a "healed wounded healer." If anything, my wounds, but even more so the wounds of those so grievously harmed by my church, stand witness to the reality of winter's promise.

For mine is a church weary and wounded, broken and bruised, humbled but somehow holy. And this is the church that I have been called to serve—to serve, but also to dream. Thus I find myself still wrapped deep within winter's dark and cold embrace, still dreaming of spring.

> In the long cold darkness of winter's night
> where truth be told while heaven waits
> where poets and prophets live to tell
> a church is reborn even as it weeps.

Notes

1. Robert Service, "The Call of the Wild," in *The Spell of the Yukon and Other Verses* (Philadelphia: Edward Stern, 1910), 31.

2. Patrick Bergquist, "A Long Dark Winter's Night," *Spiritual Life: A Journal of Contemporary Spirituality,* 53, no. 1 (Spring 2007): 38.

3. Theodore Roethke, "In a Dark Time," in *Roethke: Collected Poems* (Garden City, NY: Double Day, 1966), 239.

4. Service, "The Call of the Wild," in *The Spell of the Yukon and Other Verses*, 32.

5. Patrick Bergquist, *Fairbanks Daily News-Miner,* January 10, 2003.

6. William Shakespeare, *As You Like It*, Act 2, Scene 7.

7. Bergquist, "A Long Dark Winter's Night," 35.

8. http://www.bishop-accountability.org/AbuseTracker/.

9. Thomas Doyle, A. W. Richard Sipe, and Patrick Wall, *Sex, Priests, and Secret Codes: The Catholic Church's 2000-Year Paper Trail* (Los Angeles: Volt Press, 2007), 101.

10. http://www.snapnetwork.org/.

11. Donald Cozzens, *The Changing Face of the Priesthood: A Reflection on the Priest's Crisis of Soul* (Collegeville, MN: Liturgical Press, 2000), 9.

12. Bergquist, "A Long Dark Winter's Night," 39-40.

13. Rainer Maria Rilke, *The Sonnets to Orpheus*, trans. M. D. Herter Norton (New York: W. W. Norton, 1970), part 2, chapter 13, lines 1–4.

14. Leon Podles, *Sacrilege: Sexual Abuse in the Catholic Church* (Baltimore: Crossland Press, 2008), 280.

15. Emily Dickinson, "There's a Certain Slant of Light," in *Poems by Emily Dickinson, Three Series, Complete.*

16. Robert Frost, "Dust of Snow," in *The Poetry of Robert Frost*, ed. Edward Connery Lathem (New York: Holt, Rinehart and Winston, 1969), 221.

17. Henri Nouwen, *The Wounded Healer: Ministry in Contemporary Society* (Garden City, NY: Doubleday, 1972), 82.

18. Ibid., xvi.

19. Bergquist, *Fairbanks Daily News-Miner*, May 6, 2006.

20. Nouwen, *The Wounded Healer*, 87.

21. Ibid., 93.

22. Dylan Thomas, "This Bread I Break," in *The Poems of Dylan Thomas*, ed. Daniel Jones (New York: New Directions, 1971), 86.

23. Nouwen, *The Wounded Healer*, 89.

24. Elie Wiesel, *The Messengers of God: Biblical Portraits and Legends* (New York: Simon and Schuster, 1976), 3.

25. Nouwen, *The Wounded Healer*, 84.

26. Ibid., 94.

27. William Strode, "On a Gentlewoman Walking in the Snow," Chosen by Sir Herbert Grievson and G. Bullough, in *The Oxford Book of Seventeenth Century Verse* (London: Oxford University Press, 1966), 414.

28. Elisabeth Kübler-Ross and David Kessler, *On Grief and Grieving: Finding the Meaning of Grief Through the Five Stages of Loss* (New York: Scribner, 2005), 227.

29. Ibid., 7.

30. Ibid., 10.

31. Ibid., 15.

32. Ibid., 17.

33. Bergquist, "A Long Dark Winter's Night," 38.

34. Kübler-Ross and Kessler, *On Grief and Grieving*, 21.

35. Ibid., 22.

36. Ibid., 25.

37. Wiesel, *Messengers of God*, 203–5.

38. Kübler-Ross and Kessler, *On Grief and Grieving*, 231.

39. Nouwen, *The Wounded Healer*, 81–82.

40. Pope Benedict XVI, *Saved in Hope:* Spe Salvi (San Francisco: Ignatius Press, 2008), 77.

41. Jim Forest, "A Moslem Story," in *Peacemaking: Day by Day*, vol. 2 (Erie, PA: Pax Christi USA, 2007): 78.

42. David Toups, *Reclaiming Our Priestly Character* (Omaha: Institute for Priestly Formation, 2008), 137.

43. Ibid., 97.

44. Graham Greene, *The Power and the Glory* (New York: Penguin, 1990), 210.

45. Geoffrey Robinson, *Confronting Power and Sex in the Catholic Church: Reclaiming the Spirit of Jesus* (Collegeville, MN: Liturgical Press, 2007), 7–8.

46. Theodore Roethke, "Elegy," in *Roethke: Collected* Poems (Garden City, NY: Doubleday, 1966), 144.

47. Mary Jo Bang, "The Role of Elegy," in *Elegy* (St. Paul: Graywolf Press, 2007), 63.

48. Tim Giago, "The Mission School," in *Children Left Behind: The Dark Legacy of Indian Mission Boarding Schools* (Santa Fe: Clear Light Publishing, 2006), 15–16.

49. Oscar Wilde, "The Ballad of Reading Gaol."

50. Denise Levertov, "A Cure of Souls," in *Denise Levertov: Poems 1960–1968* (New York: New Directions, 1983), 92.

51. Toups, *Reclaiming Our Priestly Character*, 173.